Foundations of Modern Management:
Marketing

Volume 6

Edited with a new Introduction by
Morgen Witzel

OVERSTONE

Marketing

Edited and Introduced by Morgen Witzel

Printed in England by Antony Rowe Ltd., Chippenham

Marketing Research Technique

PERCIVAL
WHITE

THOEMMES PRESS

KYOKUTO SHOTEN LTD

This edition co-published in 2000 by

THOEMMES PRESS
11 Great George Street, Bristol BS1 5RR, United Kingdom

KYOKUTO SHOTEN LTD
12, Kanda-Jimbocho 2-Chome, Chiyoda-Ku, Tokyo, Japan

www.thoemmes.com

MARKETING
8 volumes : ISBN 1 85506 628 9

MARKETING RESEARCH
TECHNIQUE

MARKETING RESEARCH TECHNIQUE

BY

PERCIVAL WHITE
Percival White, Inc.
Marketing Counselors

HARPER & BROTHERS PUBLISHERS
NEW YORK AND LONDON
1931

CONTENTS

ACKNOWLEDGMENT

Particular acknowledgment is made to H. A. Haring, Jr., of Lehigh University, who is responsible very largely for the creative work.

The Arnold Research Service and R. O. Eastman, Inc., have been very helpful in supplying material.

Adolph Rebensburg, of Percival White, Inc., did much of the work of compilation. The proof reading and indexing and so forth were done by Miss Marion K. Nolan of the same organization.

PREFACE

THE primary purpose of this book is to serve as a manual of instruction for field workers. Some apparently extraneous matter has been included on the principle that an understanding of the whole subject of market analysis is essential to good field work. The material is so organized that the interviewer will be able to relate the work which he or she does to that of the survey as a whole.

A second purpose is to present to the purchasers of a market research a comprehensive description of the methods used in obtaining the practical recommendations which they desire and need. When business men understand the procedure used to obtain market facts, and the difficulties involved, they will be in a better position to know what market research can do for them, what it cannot do, and the amount of dependence which may be placed upon the facts which a survey discloses.

Throughout, the text has been illustrated with practical examples. A deliberate attempt has been made to obtain these illustrations from impartial sources and from research in which the author has not participated. An endeavor has also been made to present all of the material in a practical manner, so that the field investigator of today will have an adequate background to become the research director of tomorrow.

The author wishes to express his appreciation for assistance rendered by Department of Commerce, Washington, D. C.; Department of Agriculture, Washington, D. C.; W. J. Reilly, New York City; General Motors Corporation, Detroit, Mich.; John C. Sterling, McCall Co., New York City; Stanley I. Clark, Lehn & Fink, Inc., New York

City; Printers' Ink, New York City; Jean F. Carroll,
Meredith Publishing Co., Des Moines, Iowa; American
Telephone & Telegraph Co., New York City; Professor
Virgil Reed of Boston University; Woman's World, Chi-
cago, Ill.; Crowell Publishing Co., New York City; Lelia
Welles, New York City; E. P. Dutton & Co., Inc., New
York City; Bigelow-Sanford Carpet Co., New York City;
Babson's Statistical Organization, Wellesley Hills, Mass.;
F. C. Huyck & Sons, Albany, N. Y.; E. A. Moffatt, St.
Louis, Mo.; The Caples Co., New York City; J. Walter
Thompson Co., Chicago, Ill.; Procter & Gamble Co., Cin-
cinnati, Ohio; The Jell-O Company, Inc., New York City;
Fuller Brush Company, Hartford, Conn.

PART ONE

INTRODUCTION

Chapter I.   Development of Field Research.

Chapter II. Types of Field Research Agencies.

Chapter III. Application of Field Research.

Part One describes briefly the history of field research, the predominant types of field research organizations, and the purposes for which field research is used. An understanding of the present problems and practices of field research is facilitated through a general knowledge of the profession, hence a condensed summary of its development is presented. Modern standards of field research practice are also discussed.

The first chapter presents facts about the adaptation of scientific procedure from purely scientific research, the difficulties involved, and the attempt to reach satisfactory standards. An outline of the history of field research is also included. Chapter II deals with existing field-research agencies, the advantages and disadvantages of each type of agency, and the adequacy of the present organizations. In Chapter III a number of illustrations are presented. These show how particular firms have used research to determine their course of action and the benefits which have followed.

CHAPTER I

DEVELOPMENT OF FIELD RESEARCH

IMPORTANT decisions in business are surprisingly easy to make if all the facts are known. The Parker Pen Company believed that the public would purchase colored fountain pens and also large-sized pens. Should such pens be produced and offered to the public? If a wrong decision were made, the result might be very costly. Users of fountain pens were approached for information on the subject and the consensus of opinion was that colored and large-sized pens were desirable and would be salable. A comparatively small number of such pens were then made for use in trial markets. As these experimental sales were successful, widespread distribution was then attempted. The result was very satisfactory. The company, however, might have been wrong in its original belief, and if it had not first used field research and trial sales, might have plunged into a disastrous attempt to give the new products nation-wide distribution.

Research calls for the gathering of facts in an impartial manner. Every effort should be made to eliminate bias and prejudice and to obtain information which represents the entire general situation. Experience, widespread and of long duration, is the proper basis for determining facts. Field research collects representative information from various persons who are familiar with the particular problem under consideration, and thus gives the business executive the requisite knowledge upon which to base his judgment.

3

Many firms do not know all of the important uses to which their products are put. Under such circumstances, the "insiders" can hardly be expected to decide wisely about the best method to increase sales. Finding the uses of a product necessitates reaching a considerable sample of its consumers. Except in the case of some industrial products, individual consumers are normally approached in their respective localities. This often requires field research throughout the country to find the facts from original sources.

Brief History of Field Research.—Prior to 1910, most straight business research involved study about production. Scientific management, as advocated by Taylor, caused a considerable amount of research into methods of wage payment, time and motion study, and similar problems. Market and distribution research then began to develop, and there was a widespread interest in it. Starting in a limited way about 1910, activity in this field gradually expanded. The depression of 1921 started a phenomenal interest in marketing research. This eventually brought about the formation of a considerable number of field organizations. At present, progress in market research is continuing at a rapid rate, with no indications of abating.

Credit and statistical service bureaus are now fairly widespread. Their forces are efficient and they offer service which can be purchased at a fixed fee. Similar to these are the organizations which make up classified lists, directories of advertising agents and their clients, and supply considerable information of a similar nature presented in systematic form.

Government bureaus, universities, banks, and insurance companies gather some market data, which are made available in printed form, either at a nominal cost or free. The titles given in Fig. 1 on pages 6 and 7 indicate the type of material made available.

The preceding groups of research organizations, however, seldom investigate special problems for individual companies, but merely keep their regular information up-to-date or expand into fields of general rather than particular interest.

Research organizations which are available in solving the specific problems of individual concerns are operated by:

1. The concern itself.
2. Advertising agencies.
3. Commercial research agencies,
   Marketing counselors.
4. Publishing companies.

These channels for collecting particular market facts are now so developed that any company can obtain capable and reliable assistance from existing research agencies at a reasonable cost. This was not true in 1920, or even in 1925, but the last few years have seen great expansion on the part of trustworthy research agencies.

Standards of Field Practice.—As late as 1920, there were few, if any, well-recognized standards of practice in field research. Even today, they are by no means universally adopted. The following list shows the progress which has been made towards standardization:

1. *Interviewers.* Expert interviewers have in most cases been found to be worth their extra cost. Regardless of what the solution of the problem "ought" to be, interviewers should never be given an intimation of it. Investigators with prejudices as to the situation are to be avoided. But unbiased interviewing by skilled persons has shown excellent results.

2. *Reporting the Interview.* Memory has been found untrustworthy when recapitulating a mass of statements made during a number of interviews. An investigator, at the end

*290. Georgia School of Technology, Research Bureau (Atlanta, Ga.)—
Continued.*
  Marketing Watermelons. Preliminary report available as a
  mimeographed circular, dated March, 1928.
  Studies in progress:
    Market value of Georgia peaches by grades and sizes f. o. b.
    cars Georgia shipping points.
    Practices adapted to community cooperative assembling and
    group selling of live poultry.
  Studies contemplated for 1928:
    Practices adapted to auction selling of live hogs at shipping
    points.
    Track selling of peaches.
*291. Harvard University, Bureau of Business Research (Soldiers Field,
Mass.):*
  (Unless otherwise noted all reports were published by the Bureau
  of Business Research as bulletins. The number preceding the
  title of each report is the bulletin number.)
  Operating expenses and management problems in the retail shoe
  trade:
    1. Object and History of the Bureau, with Some Prelimi-
       nary Figures on the Retailing of Shoes. (Out of
       print.)
    2. Operating Accounts for Retail Shoe Stores.
    4. Depreciation in the Retail Shoe Business. (Out of print.)
    7. System of Stock Keeping for Retail Shoe Stores.
    10. Management Problems in Retail Shoe Stores, 1913–1917.
    20, 28, 31, 36, 43. Operating Expenses in Retail Shoe Stores.
       (1919–1923, respectively.)
  Operating expenses and management problems in the retail grocery trade:
    3. Operating Accounts for Retail Grocery Stores.
    5. Expenses in Operating Retail Grocery Stores, 1914.
    13. Management Problems in Retail Grocery Stores, 1918.
    18, 35, 41, 52. Operating Expenses in Retail Grocery Stores.
       (1919, 1922–1924, respectively.) (No. 35 out of print.)
  Operating expenses and management problems in the wholesale
  grocery trade:
    8. Operating Accounts for Wholesale Grocers.
    9. Operating Expenses in the Wholesale Grocery Business,
       1916.
    14. Methods of Paying Salesmen and Operating Expenses in
       the Wholesale Grocery Business in 1918.
    19. Operating Expenses in the Wholesale Grocery Business in
       1919.
    24. The Wholesale Grocery Business in January, 1921. (Out
       of print.)
    26, 30, 34, 40. Operating Expenses in the Wholesale Grocery
       Business. (1920–1923, respectively.) (Nos. 26 and 34
       out of print.)
    55. Cases on Merchandise Control in the Wholesale Grocery
       Business.

Operating expenses and management problems in the retail hardware trade:
    11. System of Operating Accounts for Hardware Retailers.
    12. Operating Expenses in Retail Hardware Stores, 1917–18.
    21. Operating Expenses in Retail Hardware Stores in 1918.
Operating expenses and management problems in the retail drug
trade:
    16. Operating Accounts for Retail Drug Stores.
    22. Operating Expenses in Retail Drug Stores in 1919. (Out
        of print.)
Operating expenses and management problems in the retail
jewelry trade:
    15. Operating Accounts for Retail Jewelry Stores.
    23, 27, 32, 38, 47, 54, 58, 65. Operating Expenses in Retail
        Jewelry Stores. (1919–1926, respectively.)
Operating expenses and management problems in department
stores:
    29. Explanation of Schedule for Department Stores. (Out of
        print.)
    33, 37, 44, 53, 57, 63. Operating Expenses in Department
        Stores. (1921–1926, respectively.) (No. 44 out of print.)
    59. Cases on Merchandise Control in Women's Shoe Depart-
        ments of Department Stores.
    61. Department Store Operating Expenses for 1926 and
        Financial Ratios for 1923, 1924, 1925. Preliminary
        report.

FIG. 1

A page from Market Research Agencies published by the U. S.
Department of Commerce. This shows the type of material collected and published by universities

of a day's work, will often report an erroneous consensus
of evidence because of the vividness of a few outstanding
impressions. Therefore, each interview ought to be immediately recorded in note form and written up at the
first convenient opportunity. The facts, as found, will then
be accurately recorded. The tendency is to rely more and
more upon the evidence of recorded and demonstrable
facts.

3. *Analysis of the Problem.* Originally, surveys were
often carried on with a hazy notion of exactly what information was required. Common practice now is to
analyze the specific problem and the environment in
which it is set, all parties concerned agreeing through
consultation about what facts are needed and how to

WILL YOU HELP US EDIT WOMAN'S WORLD?

ANSWER THESE QUESTIONS, PLEASE, AND RECEIVE A REWARD

We are doing our best to make Woman's World your magazine, to put into it things to interest and help you the most—to make it a source of entertainment and inspiration for the entire family and of definite, practical helpfulness for you upon whose shoulders rest the happiness and welfare of the nation's homes. But we need your help. To be of greatest service to you, we must know more about you, so if you will send us your answers to the following questions before February 15, we will send you, postpaid, as your reward, the book described below.

Cut this questionnaire out and mail it promptly to Cora F. Sanders, Woman's World, 4223 West Lake Street, Chicago, Ill.—and we will send you free, postpaid, one of the books in our new Cookery Library in full colors.

1. How many years have you been a subscriber of Woman's World?
....

2. How many members in your family?............................
Children under 10?..

3. Do you own your home?............Or do you rent?............

4. In what town do you do most of your buying?...................
(Name of town)

5. Do you live in town or on a farm?................If you live on a farm, how many miles are you from the town in which you shop? ....

6. If you live in a town, what is its population?...................

7. Please indicate below where you buy the following items. If all in one town, a simple check mark will do. If distributed between two or more places, please indicate by such words as "half," "most" or "some."

Where do you buy your: Please check in proper place	Is dealer located in your own town?	Is dealer located in neighboring town or city?	Do you buy by mail?
Furniture	....	....	....
Hardware	....	....	....
Paint	....	....	....
Silverware	....	....	....
Jewelry, watches	....	....	....
Women's clothing	....	....	....
Men's clothing	....	....	....
Children's clothing	....	....	....
Building materials	....	....	....
Groceries	....	....	....
Kitchen cabinets	....	....	....
Toilet preparations	....	....	....

8. Is there a chain grocery store in your town?...................

9. Do you own a radio set?...........If so, what make?...........
How many tubes?............Does it operate from a light plug or

from a battery?.............What make of a loud speaker do
you own? ....
Did you buy it from:
  (a) a dealer located in the town in which you live?............
  (b) a mail order house?...............................
  (c) was it made at home?........................
10. Have you electricity in your home? Yes............No..........
Have you an—
  (a) electric vacuum cleaner?.........What make?.............
  (b) electric washing machine?........What make?.............
  (c) electric refrigerator?............What make?.............
  (d) electric range?..................What make?.............
  (e) electric fan?.....................What make?.............
  (f) electric toaster?..................What make?.............
  (g) electric percolator?.............What make?.............
  (h) electric curling iron?.............What make?.............
  (i) electric heater?..................What make?.............
  (j) electric grill?...................What make?.............
  (k) electric fireless cooker?.........What make?.............
11. Please list electrical appliances purchased from:
  (a) dealer located in your own town...........................
  (b) dealer in neighboring town or city........................
  (c) office of light and power company..........................
  (d) mail order house..
12. What brand of silverware do you own?..........................
13. Did you buy from local dealer?........Mail order?..............
14. Do you intend building this year?..............
Residence?.. Garage?.. Farm building?.. Commercial building?..
What material will be used? Wood?.....Brick?.....Cement?.....
Hollow tile?.....

Please sign your name plainly below. We shall hold all replies absolutely confidential.

Name....................... R. F. D. or St. No...............
City.......................... State..........................

Cut Out This Entire Panel and Mail Before Feb. 15 to Cora F. Sanders, Woman's World, Chicago

FIG. 2

A questionnaire which was inserted in a magazine. This procedure sometimes brings excellent results

discover them, the result being accurately set forth in writing.

4. *Survey Reports*. Reports have, in the past, been of various kinds and volume. Some gave the facts alone in two hundred pages; others reduced the results to only one page. The form of presenting reports is to some extent becoming standardized—the findings and methods of procedure are summarized, usually at the beginning, and the supporting evidence is set forth in the main body of the report. Many research agencies' have also assumed the responsibility of stating what the discovered facts mean and of recommending how the discoveries may best be acted upon.

5. *Questions*. After much experimentation, it has been found that questions, in order to bring valid results, must be factual, simple, not suggestive of the desired answer, and not ambiguous.

6. *Mail Questionnaires*. A return stamped envelope should normally be inclosed. A letter of request is commonly included. Occasionally, some small reward is offered in return for properly presented information. The returns from questionnaires should average 10 per cent (or more) of the number sent out, if the work is skillfully done.

It is sometimes possible to have a magazine insert a brief questionnaire in one of its issues, with paragraph requesting readers to answer it. An example of this is given in Fig. 2 on pages 8 and 9. This is an unusual method of sending out a questionnaire, but it has been successful in some instances.

7. *Tabulation*. The basic method of treating material obtained in the field is statistical. The answers to questions are divided into classifications. For example, the question, "Have you ever used X?" would require three classifications for its answers, "Yes," "No," and "Do not know." If respondents were divided into classes according

to income, each income group would require this classification. The statistical method divides and groups the
answers to each question into many classifications and
sub-classifications, so that all of the pertinent information
can be squeezed out of the field reports in detailed form.

8. *Sample.* Not all of the consumers of an article widely
used in homes can be successfully approached. Only a
small portion can be interviewed. Many surveys of the
past have had insufficient geographic distribution; the bulk
of the people who answered the questions were sometimes
members of one particular income group; an inadequate
number of replies was frequently received. The determina-
tion of what constitutes a sufficient sample upon which to
base decisions regarding a whole group is always a problem in field research. Market areas, classifications of consumers, and the like are, however, being gradually worked
out and standardized. The sampling method needs improvement, but progress has been made.

9. *Testing and checking.* Early questionnaires were
made up in the office without any testing in the field before general use. Present practice requires that each questionnaire be tested, revised, and retested before being used.
Mail returns are sometimes checked against the results
obtained from interviewing, while experts are often consulted to learn how their beliefs agree with the facts gathered from the field. Scientific methods are followed. Every
step of the investigation is checked and, whenever possible,
the final results are tried out on a small scale before being
put into general use.

10. *Costs.* Standard accounting practice is being rapidly
developed by the leading field-research agencies. Clients
can be certain as to what expenses are included in the gross
charge for a survey. The research agencies know with
greater precision what their costs are, and prices, in general, are becoming more and more standardized. The result
is that business concerns are able to obtain similar service

from any of a number of research agencies for comparable prices.

Though considerable progress has been made, important improvements in establishing standards for marketing research are still needed, and it may be several decades before the standards will be entirely satisfactory. Such scientific procedure as exists in chemistry, for example, with its controlled laboratory conditions, will never be possible in field research, where consumers and marketing conditions cannot be arbitrarily regulated, but must be taken as they exist. On the whole, however, the accomplishments of the last ten years are noteworthy because of the initiation of standards and the adoption of a more scientific approach.

Field Work as a Training.—Field research has given to many interviewers a splendid opportunity to obtain a practical business training. Textbooks and instruction can teach theories, but varied experience is essential, in addition to technical knowledge, to a sound education.

Efficient marketing has become the aim of all manufacturers. This includes successful merchandising, advertising, selling, and distribution, all of these based upon and kept up to date by facts found through research. Any person whose aim is to enter one of these fields can have no better training than to become familiar with the practical facts and problems encountered by business firms in the marketing of their products. Most field surveys are for the purpose of solving problems which will prove recurrent in the investigator's future career. The interviewer comes into direct contact with consumers, retailers, and wholesalers. He learns their attitudes, prejudices, complaints, and troubles. He sees these as they actually exist, and can thus gain valuable experience in general business as well as in marketing.

To record properly what is learned from those approached develops ability in making accurate observations, grasping important points, and reproducing correctly from notes. It is comparable to the excellent training given by newspaper work. Directing a conversation along desired lines, so that the person interviewed does not realize that he is being led to express himself freely, calls for quick and logical thinking. The brief summary required at the end of a questionnaire is an exercise of judgment and analytical skill. The general summary, made at the end of a survey, calls for ability to analyze and digest the mass of information which has been collected. All these processes have marked educational value.

CHAPTER II

TYPES OF FIELD RESEARCH AGENCIES

FIELD research may be divided into two broad classes, one relating to *mass* information and the other to *individual* data. When, for example, studies of the resources of certain market areas are made by Chambers of Commerce, mass information is collected. As these facts are useful to many business concerns, the results usually are published, although sometimes they are given only to those who support the work. When knowledge is acquired regarding the affairs of a single company, this information is individual and specialized, and its greatest value is to the firm for which it has been collected. Therefore, in most cases, it is not available to others. The line of distinction between these two forms of work is not always sharp.

Mass surveys are conducted by many organizations. The United States Department of Commerce lists 655 organizations in the latest edition of *Market Research Agencies*, and has included none which have not made public at least some of their work. It has also endeavored to list all of the published material. The agencies are classified in the following manner:

1. Federal governments.
2. State governments.
3. Colleges, universities, and foundations.
4. Publishers of books and trade directories.
5. Commercial organizations
    Advertising agencies
    Business services
    Chambers of commerce

Cooperative marketing associations
Individual businesses
Magazines
Newspapers
Trade associations.

The various government bureaus, universities, foundations, and the like, frequently compile lists or catalogues of the material which they have available. A letter to these organizations will bring information as to the work which they have completed or expect to complete in the near future.

Individual research organizations collect some mass data and make at least a portion of the results available to the public. Only a limited group, however, is prepared to make surveys into the specific problems of a particular company. Such types are:

1. Research department of the company itself.
2. Research departments of advertising agencies.
3. Commercial research organizations.
    Marketing counselors.
4. Research departments of magazines and newspaper publishers.
5. Miscellaneous, such as departments of financial organizations.

Individual Business Research Departments.—A number of the larger corporations have established research departments of their own. Some of these, for example, are the American Multigraph Sales Company, the Chicago, Burlington & Quincy Railroad, the Dennison Manufacturing Company, the Eastman Kodak Company, the General Electric Company, the General Motors Corporation, the Metropolitan Life Insurance Company, the Stewart Warner Speedometer Corporation, Swift & Company, and the Lehn & Fink Products Company. The structural organization of one such research department is shown in Fig. 3. The research departments of a few corporations are capable of carrying on a nation-wide survey with their own personnel, but most of them delegate the greater part of the actual field work to outside agencies.

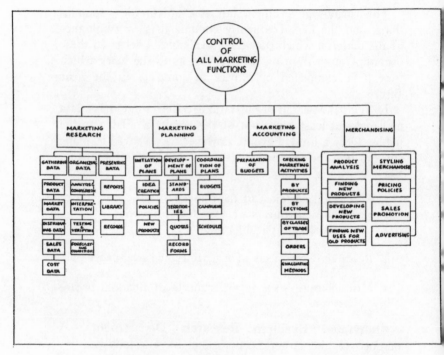

FIG. 3
Structural organization of a research department of a
large corporation

Corporations are finding it more and more desirable, however, to have one or more men continuously employed in, and responsible for, their market research. Such men are in direct contact with field work, even though done by outside services.

A business firm derives the following advantages (and possibly others) from having its own research department:

1. *Continuity of effort.* Investigation does not end with the survey and report, but further developments are continually looked for and recorded.

2. *Correlation of research.* There are certain basic principles which can be applied to all surveys and, when the information is collected by the company, all of the facts already discovered on the same subject can be fully utilized, and duplication of effort can be avoided.

3. *Access to records of company.* The chief executives are usually willing to let their own men delve into records which disclose confidential facts. This may not be true when outside organizations are employed; therefore in certain types of research, this is a deciding factor.

4. *Independence.* Outside organizations, although they may be used to supplement the company's research department, need not be allowed to impede the progress of the work. Vital problems can be given priority and procedure be varied to meet immediate requirements.

5. *Practicability of recommendation.* The research department of a business concern is in such close touch with the whole organization and its personnel, that any recommendations submitted ought to be particularly practical and easy to put into effect. It is also in a position to convince other departments about the validity of its findings through direct and continuous contact with the persons involved.

A great disadvantage of a research department in the individual business is the cost involved. Therefore, only a few relatively large corporations have, up to the present time, established them. The ordinary firm does not do sufficient research to warrant the expenditure necessary to keep a capable full-time force. As the demand for market research is increasing, more concerns are establishing their

own research departments, although many of these are
of a skeleton type.

Advertising-Agency Research Departments.—Advertising agencies do (or have done) a large volume of
field research in marketing, perhaps more than any other
type of organization. Modern agencies of even moderate
size have some sort of research departments, which conduct surveys, carry out requests of their clients for personal as well as business services, and search for facts
requested by the other departments of the agency. An
advertisement which features the research department of
an agency is given. In one day, such a research organization may start a national survey on brand preference, ferret
out an exact description of a cotton boll, check the significance of each symbol in a coat-of-arms trade-mark, and
make foreign hotel reservations for a client. Some advertising agencies have research departments, but do not do
their own field work; other agencies are equipped to undertake very ambitious surveys of national or international
scope.

The field research done by advertising agencies divides
itself into two main types—the rush survey and the planned
survey. A client may suspect that his trade-mark is being
infringed upon in a certain territory and demand a rush
survey of the situation; a new style affecting a client's
business may have started, and a hasty survey be necessary
to gauge the significance and importance of the change.
The planned survey is usually larger and more basic. In
1929, one large agency made a national survey among
automobile owners, to determine the present facts and new
trends in the purchasing of automobiles. This survey
lasted several months and was on a nation-wide basis.

Some advantages which result from having research
done by advertising agencies are:

1. *Personnel available.* The up-to-date advertising
agencies have good research departments which are ex-

perienced and accustomed to directing field surveys. There are more of these departments than of any other type of market-research organization. Rush jobs are common and can ordinarily be pushed through satisfactorily.

2. *Impartial point of view.* Outsiders naturally have an impartial attitude towards a vital problem and this is sometimes of great value. When executives within a firm differ in opinion about the solution of a problem, an outside group ought to collect the facts.

3. *Lower cost.* Serving numerous clients, the research department of an agency can be of considerable size and yet have a relatively low cost per survey or per interview, due to dividing the overhead between the several surveys or projects undertaken. Most corporations can have all necessary field research done at a much lower cost in this manner than by establishing an adequate department for themselves.

4. *Free market research.* This is sometimes offered by advertising agencies. In the case of large accounts, it is considered justifiable to include some market research as a part of the ordinary service offered. On the other hand, if the agency can afford to conduct free surveys without extra commission, it is sometimes suspected of being overpaid when it does not do this. Free surveys which encroach upon the normal profits of the agency are bad business.

Agencies frequently conduct field surveys to obtain facts which are essential to performing the service for which they are retained. These are in no sense "free surveys." Frequently it is impossible to tell whether or not a survey ought to be considered an extra service for the client. Often both types of data are gathered and the cost of the survey might well be split between the agency and its client.

The disadvantages which may arise from having research done by advertising agencies are:

1. *Lack of continuity.* Surveys are conducted for numerous clients. When a specific task has been completed, other facts are usually not acquired until a new survey is ordered. With a change of advertising agents, the client loses some of the continuity with the research work previously done for him.

2. *Confidential problems.* Some problems are considered too confidential to delegate to outside organizations.

3. *Bias.* The agency research department has a dual allegiance, being responsible to both the client and the agency. This may influence the interpretation of data and facts because the agency makes its main income from discounts upon the advertising space purchased.

4. *Limited choice.* Advertising agencies do not ordinarily conduct surveys for concerns unless they also handle their advertising.

Commercial Research Organizations. The number of commercial research organizations specializing in field work has increased somewhat during the last few years, but the volume of work which they have done has increased more than has the number of such bureaus.

Commercial research organizations are employed by business firms, either directly or through their advertising agents. Some corporations have all their research done in this manner. Others use these organizations to supplement their own research work or to compare with the information gained through their advertising agents.

Large corporations with skilled personnel check and supplement work by using the facilities offered by both advertising agents and commercial research organizations.

Since the author himself is connected with an organization of the latter type, he is not in an unbiased position, but to him the commercial research organization appears to offer the following advantages to a business concern:

1. *Personnel.* A permanent personnel is available which has experience and skill in market research.

2. *Point of view.* An outside organization approaches a problem without bias. The personnel is trained to do impartial work. In some problems this is of the utmost importance.

3. *Cost.* It is usually less expensive to employ a commercial research organization than to establish a research department, because the organization has a greater volume of work, hence the overhead for any individual survey is less.

4. *Undivided allegiance.* The research organization profits through turning out first-class research work. There is no divided allegiance, as is said sometimes to be true in the case of the advertising agency.

5. *Service.* Research is the primary occupation of the organization. Prompt service and attention may be expected. If such is not forthcoming, or cannot be promised, the business firm can have its survey made by a competitive organization. In the case of the advertising agency, it is sometimes very difficult to avoid transferring the advertising account as well as the survey, if trouble is had with the latter.

Some disadvantages of the commercial research agency may be:

1. *Confidential problems.* Some problems are considered too confidential to give to outsiders.

2. *Lack of continuity.* Surveys are commonly not authorized until a problem has become pressing. This causes too little research to be done, and what is actually done would usually have been more valuable if completed sooner. This, however, is not the fault of the research agency, because it would be glad to furnish periodic service for any reputable concern.

"Too Confidential" Attitude Disappearing.—General Motors Corporation has good market-research facilities, yet it annually has considerable market-research work done by outside organizations. This is a fairly typical case. Confidence in the integrity of advertising and commercial research organizations is becoming widespread. All facts, reports, tabulations, and the like, which are obtained during an individual survey, are considered by these research organizations to be the property of their clients. One commercial-research organization goes so far as to state that it will not undertake surveys in the same competitive field for different clients unless the first survey is at least two years old and the original client states that he does not wish to bring the data up-to-date. Even then, none of the information collected during the first survey is used.

Market-research organizations are beginning to establish themselves in an advisory capacity, similar to that held by law firms. Many large corporations have legal departments of their own, yet they invariably call in outside law firms on important cases. Nothing is too confidential to place in the hands of a reputable lawyer. Within the next few years, market-research organizations ought to have reached a similar position. Even now, many business firms are giving the free access to their records. The connection between research organizations and business firms is beginning to have a more permanent aspect.

Magazine and Newspaper Publishers.—Magazine and newspaper publishers collect numerous mass data concerning markets. Some of this work is exceedingly well done. The Crowell Publishing Company, for example, annually compiles an excellent volume entitled *National Markets and National Advertising* (see Fig. 4 on page 23). The *Detroit News* has published a "Salesmen's Retail Route List" and a "Salesman's Map of Detroit." The foregoing are rather typical of the work done by large magazine publishers and metropolitan newspapers. Some mass information, however, is open to the charge of bias because of the intent of such companies to sell advertising space. The

This volume is the sixth edition of National Markets and National Advertising.

For five years past The Crowell Publishing Company has made some form of market study. In each case our effort has been to develop a market measure that would assist both the advertiser and his agent to determine the potential business which the market offered.

For the last two years this market measure has been stated in terms of income. Our study demonstrated to us that this was one of the most valuable pieces of information about each market area available for judging past sales efforts and determining future sales possibilities.

A new set of income figures has not been developed for this volume. The past year has not produced enough new basic data to justify a revision of the previous figures and, moreover, the figures in last year's book still come within a few per cent of being as useful and as accurate a market measurement as they were last year.

But any statistical expression of a market is necessarily one dimensional. Only its *length* is indicated. Its other dimensions must be measured. It is one thing to know that a certain size market exists; it is quite another to reach it.

Yet markets are sold and skilfully sold. And no other agency for reaching the national market has yet proved so effective as the national magazine.

But why is this so? Why has the national magazine been such an able ally of American business?

One would expect to find a whole literature treating of this subject. Oddly enough there is no full statement of what the national magazine is and what it has done. In bits and by piecemeal, various phases, uses and trends of the national magazine have been written down or recited, but never has anything like a complete story been told in one place.

This is what The Crowell Publishing Company has attempted in the present volume. This study is devoted to clarifying and illustrating the relationship which has existed between the national magazine and the unification of customers, ideas and manners in America.

FIG. 4

Foreword from *National Markets and National Advertising*, published by the Crowell Publishing Company

Association of National Advertisers selects the dependable work of publishers and keeps this on file for its members. On the whole, the more recent researches have been the most reliable.

Publishing companies, especially newspaper publishers, have made individual surveys for prospective or actual buyers of advertising space. In some cases, valuable information on individual or brand problems may be obtained. To facilitate the gathering of such data, newspapers in various cities have banded themselves together. The Rodney E. Boone Organization, for example, represents sixteen newspapers in ten major cities. A questionnaire given to the Boone papers will be used in all ten cities. No great number of calls can be made in any one city, but a few can be expected.

Mr. John C. Sterling, vice-president of the McCall Company, has stated that "the publisher never has been and never will be qualified to investigate an individual advertiser's own product. The publisher, of course, is not familiar with its history or problems."

The individual work of the publishers should not be overlooked, however, as a means of supplementing and checking data obtained through a field survey. The main point is to avoid depending too much upon such information.

Newspapers, in many cases, can assist a market survey in several ways, as by:

1. Mass surveys of market conditions.
2. Route lists.
3. Information maps.
4. Reviews of business conditions.
5. Merchandising field calls.

Aid in all of these directions should be taken advantage of, yet it should be fully realized that the function of the newspaper or local publisher is to facilitate and expedite market research rather than to conduct it.

CHAPTER III

APPLICATION OF FIELD RESEARCH

FIELD research has been used to gather many types of facts. From this material practical business policies have been developed. The following cases have been taken from reputable public sources, so that there can be no question concerning them. More striking examples could unquestionably be presented by choosing unusual illustrations rather than those of a more common nature. This has not been done because field research will, in the end, stand or fall by its success in solving the problems of successful concerns.

1. *The Lewis Manufacturing Company.*[1] The Lewis Manufacturing Company, a division of the Kendall Company, manufactures "Curity" cheesecloth. The company's market-research department was given the task of discovering what could be done to improve distribution. An investigation yielded the fact that there were more than one hundred uses of cheesecloth. By studying retail sales figures, by examining the company's books, and by talks with consumers and retailers, it was discovered that there are really two general classes of uses which require two different types of "Curity" cheesecloth.

The first class is the dusting, cleaning, and polishing use which requires a cheesecloth of open construction, a cheap fabric which can be used a few times and thrown away. The other class is the general household use of cheesecloth for such purposes as jelly-strainers, lettuce bags, cold-cream removers, etc. These require a finer-count

[1] *Printers' Ink*, March 6, 1930, p. 126.

cloth. The market-research department also found facts which proved that cheesecloth for each of these general purposes must be merchandised separately because there is really a separate market for each.

The company was forced to recognize that its two market problems were tied up with packaging; therefore it created two grades of packaged cheesecloth to satisfy the demands of the two markets it discovered. In addition, two counter containers were developed to overcome the difficulty that cheesecloth is seldom displayed. Each container holds a dozen packages and each carries a picture showing the uses of the particular grade which it holds.

The facts found by the market-research department caused these changes while the changes themselves offered a fine selling argument. A typical advertisement to the trade called, "The Curity Two Market Selling Method" reads:

Here is an idea, and a method of capitalizing it, that will increase your cheesecloth sales. The cheesecloth market is really divided into two sharply defined parts. One covers the personal and kitchen uses, for which the finer-weave cheesecloth is necessary. The other covers general cleaning, dusting, and polishing uses for the car and home, for which the lower-count, open-weave cheesecloth is more suitable. Curity furnishes a method of covering both these with a separate and distinct package and display for each. The display on the left, for the finer weaves, holds nine-inch or eighteen-inch packages. One dozen nine-inch packages of open-weave cheesecloth are shipped in the carton on the right, which becomes a display when opened as shown. You are not taking full advantage of existing cheesecloth markets unless you have both of these displays on your counter. Write to your jobber or to us for yours today.

2. *A manufacturer with a big line.*[1] Recently a manufacturer with a large line of merchandise wondered whether

[1] *Printers' Ink*, February 6, 1930, p. 166.

he was pushing the correct items as leaders. He asked each salesman to get from every one of his retail customers a list of ten regular and representative users of the company's long line of products. In a few weeks he thus secured a list of 500 good names in different parts of the territories that were served. Then this simple letter was drafted:

DEAR CUSTOMER:

Your name has been given to us by . . . as a regular user of several of our products in our complete line. We are glad to take this opportunity of thanking you for your past patronage, and are also asking you in our first letter to do us a favor and help us solve a problem.

On a separate sheet we have listed our entire line of thirty-eight separate items with a voting square opposite each. Will you, as a personal favor to us, mark down a number opposite the five items you would want us to keep in case we discontinued all the other items in the line? We are seriously considering the idea of dropping all except five products, and are coming direct to you to aid us in their selection. We don't want to stop making your favorite. Will you please indicate in order the five you want us to keep? This action would be greatly appreciated.

Sincerely yours,

P.S.—We shall be much pleased to send each voter a sample box of our latest product.

The letter gave the company a chance to tell 500 customers, many of whom used only a few of its items, about its entire line and at the same time to get a direct answer to the "leader" problem. The company received 297 replies from the 500 letters and the results were surprising. Five points was given an item for a first choice, three for a second choice, etc., so that the tabulation would be comprehensive. When the votes were counted, the winner was found to be a product made by all of the firm's big competitors, but never pushed by any of its makers, being considered, in fact, a sort of staple. Retailers had been asked to supply a list of the ten items which they considered best as leaders, yet neither the winner nor the runner-up appeared on the dealer lists.

Many customers, in addition to furnishing the desired information, wrote in about articles in the long line with which they were not familiar. These letters were answered and inquiries turned over to retailers, causing sales on the whole line to jump and remain high.

In spite of the fact that consumer votes indicated an article which surprised both the company and its retailers, it was decided to follow the facts found by the questionnaire. The item was then improved, a new package and design created, and preparations made for featuring the new leader in newspaper advertising. The first advertisement was reprinted and mailed with a letter to the list of 500 customers (who had received the original inquiry letter), whether they had answered or not, telling them that here was the new item they had helped to choose. After six months the old trailer picked by the firm's customers as the new leader had turned out very well in its new rôle. Distribution was at first pushed in only one state, but rapidly spread to include nine states, and plans have been made to further increase this area. An executive of the company expressed himself in the following manner about the effects of the new leader :

Results have shown in many other ways. Not only have we increased the radius of our sales activities and added a large number of new accounts, but we have cut selling costs on our whole line. Our plan aroused real interest not only among the customers whose names the retailers gave us, but among our whole sales force. The plan gave us a real advertisable leader for which there was a latent demand not realized by either ourselves or our big competitors, and also helped sales on every item in our line.

3. *A New England Manufacturer.*[1] A prominent New England concern manufactures many products going through the same channels of distribution, namely, the hardware, drug, and stationery trades. As new products were added to the line, the company expected that New England would contribute a large volume of business. For several years, on the contrary, business in New England declined in comparison with the rest of the United States.

This unsatisfactory condition led to a special study of the New England territory. A competent investigator traveled throughout the six states for six weeks, calling on jobbers and dealers in almost every line and studying methods used by companies whose products were selling successfully in New England. He learned that certain manufacturers were using specialized selling policies there which were selling well, those which were not, and the reasons, if they could be discovered. He learned which manufacturers were selling direct to the retail trade only, which were selling through jobbers only, and which were selling to both the retailers and the jobbers, and the results in each case.

He asked the jobbers' frank opinion as to whether the forty-year-old policy of the company in selling exclusively through jobbers was right under present conditions. He found out from retailers whether they preferred to purchase direct from the manufacturer or through jobbers. Having obtained this information, he called upon manufacturers who were known to use special distribution policies in New England or whose products were leaders in the field.

The main conclusion from the investigation was that jobbers, by their own candid admission, were handicapped

---

[1] Report No. 5—"Use of Research in Sales Management"—prepared for the Research Committee of the New England Council by the Policyholders Service Bureau of the Metropolitan Life Insurance Company, p. 7.

in their attempts to introduce new products, regardless of their desire to cooperate with the manufacturer. The recommendation of the jobbers was that, since their own salesmen, by the very character of their work, were unable to do promotion work on new products, or to secure distribution for them in any considerable number of instances, manufacturers should do the introductory work themselves. The jobbers hoped that, when the manufacturers had done this, the missionary orders would be turned over to them to fill. Many jobbers said that they would respect the judgment of any manufacturer who sent his salesmen direct to the retail trade and filled orders direct, but they suggested that the manufacturer also offer his goods to the jobber, so that the jobber might have the advantage of repeat sales from such dealers, or, if the manufacturer sold exclusively to the retail trade, that, when distribution had been developed, the business be turned over to the jobbers.

As a result of this investigation, the company decided that it could obtain the desired results by opening accounts with the retail trade and filling orders direct, continuing meanwhile to do business with the jobbers. Jobbers were urged to stock the goods that were being sold by the retail salesmen in order not only to get independent distribution, but also to fill repeat orders after the company's salesmen had established the product. The company sells to the retailer at retail discounts, with no advantage in price over what the jobber would quote. This is the only protection for which the jobber asks. Seven salesmen were sent out in New England as a result of this survey. They are supervised by a salesmanager and the plan has worked successfully for several years, although the company has no force of men selling direct to retailers in any other territory. Credit losses have been small, salesmen's volume of business has been satisfactory, and, surprisingly, business through jobbers has steadily increased.

4. *Bigelow-Sanford Carpet Company, Inc.*[1] During

---

[1] *Printers' Ink*, December 26, 1929, p. 114.

the last few years, the Bigelow-Sanford Carpet Company has endeavored to improve its sales by helping its dealers to sell rugs. It has created a monthly newspaper containing all of the newest ideas in manufacturing and retailing floor coverings, it has completely renovated its styling, and it has worked up a comprehensive method course for retail salesmen in floor-covering departments, emphasizing methods of tying floor coverings in with other store merchandise. Not satisfied with these improvements, the company decided to learn what the dealer considered his problems to be. During the 1929 fall opening in the company's New York showroom, a nation-wide survey was announced. The information obtained and its applications were to be published and distributed free to store executives, merchandise managers, etc., in monthly bulletins. The announcement was enthusiastically received by buyers and executives who attended the opening.

The survey had five parts: (a) A first-hand study of floor-covering department operation and management. (b) Questionnaires on the subject of special phases of floor-covering merchandising sent to selected lists of buyers and executives. (c) Interviewing decorators, designers, and style experts on style trends. (d) Conferring with representatives of other branches of the home-furnishing field. (e) Studying methods employed in other lines of business to meet problems like those in the floor-covering trade.

In order to limit the survey, a list of fifteen topics was submitted to a vote of a representative list of floor-covering executives. A response of one-third was received and the following topics ranked as most important:

1. Practical means of increasing rate of stock turnover.
2. {
   Modern methods of stock control.
   Reducing mark-down to a minimum.
   How to anticipate style trends.
   Displaying rugs and carpets to build sales.
   How to insure successful advertising of floor coverings.
   }

Some of the findings of the survey are of general interest. Only the most progressive and successful stores were visited, yet only 18 per cent were using sales records to guide the selection and purchase of rugs and carpets, the balance relying solely on memory, habit, and hunch of the buyers. Only 23 per cent were using any form of unit control, while less than a third of these stores had set up a "model" or "balanced" stock. It was also disclosed that most of these stores were using more progressive merchandising methods in other departments, particularly in the women's wear and shoe sections. Likewise, it was learned that the floor-covering department was being slighted in many stores with respect to window displays, advertising allotment, and the like.

When the research had been completed, the company prepared its series of reports for floor-covering department executives, advisers, buyers, etc. The first of these, for example, was called, "Planning for Speeding Up Turnover." In the trade advertising this material is being followed up through full-page space. The company has, therefore, learned what the retailers wished to know about merchandising, found the facts about such topics, analyzed and written up these facts in practical form, distributed them to the trade, and advertised this service to improve merchandising practice. The consumer campaign, which also was released in the fall of 1929, emphasized style in floor coverings, a subject which the investigation had covered. Retailers were then supplied with small style handbooks so that the consumer demand would be handled according to the suggested merchandising policies. From the very first, the results of this comprehensive merchandising policy have been very favorable.

5. *Corning Glass Works*.[1] In preparation for its 1926 advertising campaign, the Corning Glass Works decided that the market facts about Pyrex ovenware were essential.

[1] *Printers' Ink*, July 8, 1926, p. 25.

Accordingly, investigators were sent to representative towns in the East, the Midwest, and the South. For eight months these field workers studied the problems of why people purchased Pyrex and how they used it. Three additional facts were also investigated: 1. What percentage of homes used Pyrex. 2. What dishes were most frequently used. 3. What foods were most frequently used in the most popular dishes.

Interviews were had in 3,448 homes. Pyrex was owned in 68 per cent of these homes. Sales analysis showed that 82 per cent of Pyrex business was in five specified dishes; so investigators were sent into homes where 8,516 dishes of these five types were owned. This disclosed that 35 per cent owned pie plates, 25 per cent casseroles, 25 per cent custard cups, 13 per cent bread pans, and 2 per cent utility dishes, and these results checked closely with the sales analysis. The survey also showed that the five big selling dishes would accomplish almost every baking task; therefore the unavoidable conclusion was that the advertising should emphasize these five dishes alone, with the purpose of introducing Pyrex into the 32 per cent of the homes where it was not owned, and of inducing the owners of one dish to buy the four other popular types.

Surprisingly definite answers were received as to the kinds of food usually prepared in each type of dish. For example, the most popular uses of the utility dishes were for baking stuffed peppers and apples. Data were also obtained as to seasonal uses. In fact, the findings concerning uses of the product furnished unusually adequate illustrative material for the advertisements.

Tabulation of the interviews showed that 61 per cent of the women purchased Pyrex because of its better baking qualities, 41 per cent because it was easy to keep clean, 33 per cent because it could be used for baking and serving, 29 per cent because it was more attractive, and 7 per cent because it was more durable. (Percentages total over 100 per cent because all reasons given were listed and some women gave two or more reasons.)

From the above facts, the Corning Glass Works was able to write advertising copy, arrange for illustrations, choose "leaders," etc., upon the basis of proved facts. The problem of how to present the fact that Pyrex had better baking qualities than its competitors was solved by editorial copy explaining the results of actual tests by an impartial third party. The advertising campaign of 1926, worked out in accordance with these facts, yielded more inquiries in six months than were received during 1925. Later, actual sales proved that the research had been a most profitable investment, and the company has since done similar research periodically in order to keep its information up to date.

7. *Pinaud.*[1] The House of Pinaud has distributed its products in the United States for two generations. Up to 1915 all of the items in the line had shown a consistent increase in sales. From 1915, however, toilet water and hair tonic alone showed sales expansion, while the other items consistently decreased in spite of the fact that total cosmetic sales in the United States were expanding greatly. An investigation was made and the causes of this situation were found to be: 1. The war, which disrupted the Pinaud staff. 2. Increased advertising behind toilet water and hair tonic to the exclusion of other items. 3. Association of Pinaud toilet water and hair tonic with barber-shop outlets, causing a loss of prestige and refusal of numerous other outlets to carry the articles.

It was decided to expand the line to cover its proper field, cosmetics, and to give the line a quality appeal. A new factory and offices were built and a new type of cold cream developed. Likewise, a new package was designed with the purpose of creating a quality atmosphere. A brief

---

[1] *Printers' Ink*, March 6, 1930, p. 112.

description of this container indicates the care, research, and testing which were used:

A green jar was picked after much experimenting. To maintain the effective basic green background, the jar top was held in place by green silk-covered wire bound four times around the base and top and kept in place by four notches. A very simple silver-and-black harmonizing label was pasted on the jar, a silver-and-black booklet was placed opposite, and around these was wrapped a strip of transparent paper through which the basic green color could penetrate easily. Simple and colorful, this package had all the quality appeal the company desired.

Introduction to consumers was begun slowly. To determine women's reactions to the new cream, the company did sampling in summer resorts to see just how much interest might be expected. This sampling showed that the cream had wide appeal, for inquiries came from scattered sections of the country where women could have learned about the cream only as a result of the demonstrations at resort towns.

Tests were then made in small cities, and then larger ones, demonstrating and sampling going on at the same time that advertising appeared in rotogravure space ranging from one-half to full pages for from two to seven insertions. As a result of these careful tests which covered the United States broadly, Pinaud entered the New York market in January, 1928.

The results of the successful début of the new cream were, according to Mr. Quinn of Pinaud, the following:

In effect, the new cream package increased our distribution not only for itself, but for other Pinaud products. For where heretofore many of the highest-grade stores would not handle our hair tonic or toilet water, these same stores were attracted by the Pinaud quality-cream package and not only took on the cream, but also took on the toilet water and tonic as well. The net of this was not only (1) widespread outlets for the new cream, but also (2) new outlets for the old products along with (3) a growing prestige for those products which before had been associated so largely with the barber shops.

After the cream had been given sufficient time to establish itself firmly in the market, a shampoo was added to the line. In 1929, Pinaud's powder was also introduced. These products have replaced old ones of the same type in the Pinaud line, and have caused the company to produce only one cream, for example, instead of many. All of these new products are fully modernized (March, 1930) and more items may be added in the future. The shampoo and powder were introduced by the same experimental demonstration-sampling methods as the cream, except that, in the case of the powder, New York City was the first market to be entered.

8. *Mazda Lamp Merchandising Policy Tested Before Adoption.*[1] The fact that the buying public is becoming more and more educated in the buying of commodities carrying a bargain appeal for quantity purchases is evidenced in the prices of most low-priced items of merchandise. In the grocery, tobacco, toilet article, confectionery, haberdashery, and household-equipment fields consumers have been accustomed to purchasing their requirements in quantity lots, particularly wherever a price inducement has been offered.

Today, the housewife entering a grocery store does not ask for one, two or three eggs; she buys a dozen or more. She usually purchases a half-dozen bars of soap at a time. In the haberdashery store, a man usually buys three collars for a dollar; and manifests the same tendency in his purchases of neckties, socks, shirts, and other low-priced articles of apparel.

In a test recently conducted in several agents' stores, where a 10 per cent discount was offered customers on unit purchases of six or more lamps in order to determine

[1] *Printers' Ink*, August 21, 1930, p. 122.

the sales advantage of a price concession to the ultimate consumer, it was conclusively proved that a price concession will unquestionably sell more lamps per customer. The results of the test are given as follows:

1. One thousand customers bought lamps. Of these, 865 had come in to buy lamps, while 135 had not originally intended to purchase them.

2. Of the 1,000 customers who bought lamps, 390, or 39 per cent, bought in lots of six or more.

3. The total number of lamps sold was 5,000, of which 3,250, or 65 per cent, were sold at a discount of 10 per cent.

4. The average number of lamps per customer who came in to buy one, two, or three lamps, was increased from 1.68 to 2.84.

These figures are significant. They bring home the buying habits of the consuming public, which is quick to respond to a price appeal, particularly when it accompanies the offer of standard merchandise of known quality.

For years, it has been the custom of progressive Mazda lamp merchandisers to emphasize the sale of lamps by the carton. Carton sales mean greater volume, with resultant all-around benefit. To the central station they mean the filling of empty sockets, thus insuring a stability of residential lighting revenue.

The advantages of buying by the carton, of keeping spare lamps on hand, have been recited to customers through the spoken and printed word for some years. And in the majority of cases these arguments have proved convincing because they were basically sound, justified as they were from the standpoint of the consumer's best interests.

Under the new 10-per-cent-discount plan the appeal of price, the potent "pocketbook" appeal, now enters the lamp-sales picture. It is estimated that within two or three years, under the stimulus of this 10-per-cent-discount plan, the greater proportion of all lamp sales will be carton sales. Whether this actually eventuates or not depends, of course, upon the pressure that is put behind the idea by those who come into direct contact with the public.

9. *An E. P. Dutton & Co., Inc. Merchandising Plan.*[1] In the case of E. P. Dutton & Co., the "fan" customer offered an idea which has already increased the sale of the Dutton mystery books by approximately 31 per cent and promises to do even better in the months to come. The plan in which the Dutton mystery monster is the trade-mark (see Fig. 5 on page 39) and moving character came as a direct result of interviewing fan customers. What was the prime motive, the publisher and his advertising agent wondered, in influencing the fan, the real mystery fan, to buy book after book in which some detective unraveled a baffling mystery? Names of real fans were secured from booksellers and further names were obtained from among the publisher's acquaintances. It was found that a real fan wanted two things. He was interested in having mystery stories contain living people as well as dead ones, and most of all he bought mystery stories because he put himself in the position of the amateur detective and wondered whether he could have done as good a job. It was his custom, so many of the fans said, to stop at a certain portion of the book and wonder whether he could guess ahead to the correct solution.

As is usual in such investigations, this one led to a real advertising idea as well as to a change in the product. It enables the publisher to use full-page newspaper advertising headed, "A New Idea That Makes the Reading of Mystery Stories More Fascinating Than Ever." "You have often stopped in the reading of mystery stories," says the copy, "to try to determine the guilty person. Now you can do just that on a planned basis with all the clues presented and a reward for you if you determine the guilty person or persons correctly."

The details were then given; namely, that the Dutton

[1] *Printers' Ink*, November, 1930, p. 94.

clue mysteries were published with a special page inserted
in each book at a point where all the characters and necessary clues had been presented to make it possible for the

FIG. 5

Dutton mystery monster trade-mark designed because of the facts
found from mystery "fans"

reader to select the guilty person. This page pictures a
shrouded monster in a mask, holding up blood-red hands,
saying, "Stop." "Now," says the page, "do a little personal
detective work. Now you enter the story." The thought

was put up to the reader's sense of good sportsmanship not to read any further, but to select whom he thought was guilty, write the name on a coupon attached to the page, give reasons for his selection, and mail the coupon in to the publisher. If he names the guilty person correctly the publisher mails him a card certifying to that effect. He was further told that if and when he correctly named the guilty person in any three mysteries and had received three cards certifying to that fact, he would receive the next mystery book free. On the coupon attached to the idea page was a place for the reader to write in the name of his bookseller, if he wanted him to send the mystery, or a place to check for the publisher to do the same thing.

The campaign suggested by the research accomplished five distinct objectives:

1. It caused each reader of a Dutton Clue Mystery who solved one correctly to come back and attempt to solve two more correctly, in order to get the fourth free.

2. It automatically raised the unit of sale, as many dealers suggested purchasing two or three at a time.

3. It caused many repeat sales.

4. It tied the complete group up as a family of products, each gaining accumulative value and good will from the advertising and books previously published.

5. The return cards with the solution gave the publisher an excellent mailing list.

The publishers report that out of the total number of readers only 78 sleuths ran down the murder in the first book; 147 in the second, and up to this time 123 detectives have unraveled the web in the third. But—and this is a fine tribute to the sporting instinct of mystery-story readers —only one person solved all three mysteries correctly and thus received a book. The publishers also report that the idea has increased their sale of these mystery books 31 per cent up to this time.

Results Obtainable from Field Research.—The examples which have been given illustrate a few of the facts which are obtainable through field research. They also illustrate the practical applications which analysis of the facts show. The list which follows is not inclusive, but indicates the major types of facts which field research is able to gather. Practical examples of each of these will be given later in the appropriate sections of this book. Facts are found about:

1. *Markets and their potentialities.* The market and its location can be clearly defined. Likewise, its potentialities and how to realize these can be learned.

2. *Consumers.* Who they are, where they live, their buying habits, etc., can be found.

3. *Dealers.* Present dealers can be checked up; the best type of dealer can be determined; the methods used by dealers can be found.

4. *Selling policies.* The correctness of present policies, the improvement of policies, and the testing of proposed policies can all be determined.

5. *Sales territories.* The present territories are analyzed and the best territorial divisions indicated; routing in the territories can be worked out.

6. *Sales quotas.* The correct facts upon which to base the sales quota can be found and a scientific quota developed.

7. *Merchandising policies.* The policies needed can be found; old policies can be judged; proposed changes can be tested.

8. *Products.* Desirable new products can be discovered; the best sizes, prices, and qualities of a product can be determined. All of these can be given a thorough test. The uses of a product and improvements of it can be found.

9. *Packages.* Appropriate packages can be designed and tested.

10. *Trade-marks and slogans.* A tentative list can be

created and the appropriate ones tested so that the best is chosen.

11. *Advertising*. The efficiency of advertising can be determined; window displays, etc., can be tested.

12. *Copy appeals*. The reasons why people buy the product and prefer the firm can be found; most frequent uses of the product can be discovered.

13. *Magazines*. The magazines and newspapers read by consumers and retailers can be learned.

14. *Competition*. Policies, practices, etc., of competitors with the strength and weakness of each competitor's position can be determined.

15. *Persons*. Facts can be learned about any particular person or particular group of people.

Field research not only can find any or all of the above facts, but also, when in quest of specific information, usually discovers additional material of significance. All of the data are then tabulated, analyzed, and carefully studied, so that the findings take the form of practical business policies based upon organized facts which furnish proof that the policies are correct.

PART TWO

THE NATURE OF FIELD INVESTIGATION

CHAPTER IV. MARKET ANALYSIS.

CHAPTER V. PROCESSES OF RESEARCH.

CHAPTER VI. FIELD RESEARCH AND ITS PRACTICE.

Part Two explains the methods used in field research. It deals primarily with the steps involved in all scientific procedure. It also describes the application of this procedure to problems of commercial research. The field worker and the executive receiving the results of field research are both helped by a knowledge of the processes by which "raw data" from the field are turned into practical business policies.

Chapter IV describes market-analysis procedure and tells how the problem is broken down into its separate elements. In Chapter V the methods used to determine the facts required to solve scientific problems are explained. The last chapter in this section compares the various means of obtaining raw material from the field and indicates what type of information is best obtained by each of the better-known methods.

CHAPTER IV

MARKET ANALYSIS

MARKET analysis is the application of scientific principles and methods to problems connected with the nature, extent, and peculiarities of the market, together with the means for bringing the product to the market and distributing it there.

Every science is built on facts. Therefore, the first step in the application of science to markets is to learn all the pertinent facts that it is possible to obtain. First, the market facts must be obtained; second, they must be analyzed and interpreted; and third, conclusions must be drawn, checked, and applied to the particular business in question. An outline of market analysis procedure is presented at the end of this chapter. (See Fig. 9, pages 56 and 57.)

Classes of Market Data.—Market data are divided into the following main classes:

1. Bibliographical.
2. Expert.
3. Wholesale.
4. Retail.
5. Consumer.

Each of these has broad scope and will be separately outlined.

1. *Bibliographical data.* Written data are obtained from company records, books, periodicals, statistics, and other sources, such as catalogues, pamphlets, monographs, and association reports. Public, company, and technical libraries are the basic sources for books and periodicals. The libraries

have indexes for the books, and usually the *Technical Arts Index,* the *Readers' Guide to Periodical Literature,* and the

---

BIBLIOGRAPHICAL PROCEDURE
OUTLINE

1. Sources of information
    Libraries,
        public
        private
        technical or scientific
    Government
    Publicity literature, catalogues, pamphlets, etc.

2. Books
    On the industry in general
    On the product
    On merchandising methods (sales, distribution, or
        publicity)
        for the product
        for similar products

3. Periodical literature
    Trade papers and periodicals
    General periodicals
    Unusual periodicals—see *Readers' Guides*

4. Statistical information
    Government
    Libraries with statistical departments
    Statistical bureaus
    Trade associations and periodicals
    Newspapers

5. Other written information
    Catalogues
    Pamphlets, monographs, etc.

FIG. 6
An outline of bibliographical procedure

Index to Chemical Abstracts offer means of determining the location of articles in periodicals applying to the specific product in question. (Fig. 6 on page 46 presents an outline of bibliographical procedure.)

Government publications fall into many classes. The best plan is to get into direct touch with the government departments likely to have information of a desirable nature. Trade-association reports and private organization work may sometimes be obtained. Trade journals are valuable sources of material, as are such statistical organizations as Babson, the Harvard Economic Service, and the Standard Statistics Service, Inc. *Printers' Ink* keeps an index of articles published in its two magazines and is able to compile bibliographies from this upon request.

Written data give the investigator a view of what facts are already known. This is a great help, tends to avoid duplication of effort, and makes a good foundation for further research. One fault of written data is that they are not up-to-date. Books may be several years old and great changes may have taken place since they were written. In some lines of business, experience only one year old may be antiquated.

2. *Expert data.* Authorities on a subject, such as technical experts, trade papers, trade associations, chambers of commerce, etc., are approached through personal interviews or mail questionnaires, except for general data already available. Information relative to the condition of affairs in the industry, its prospects, improvement in the product, seasonal and cyclical variations of the industry, etc., can commonly be obtained. Specific answers to particular problems can also be secured in some cases. This information pertains particularly to trends within the industry and its market. It is important as a comparison with that obtained from other sources.

3. *Jobbers.* Jobbers are practical men and can give practical information if correctly solicited. Those who handle the product, or might do so, can be approached through questionnaire or interview. Jobbers, as a rule, will not give

WOOLEN BLANKET SURVEY
WHOLESALE QUESTIONNAIRE

Name of Wholesale Firm.....................................

Address...........................Type of Jobber..........

I. STOCK
1. In order of sales importance, what makes of blankets do you handle?

Brand	Imported	Wool			Cotton	
		Light	Med.	Heavy	Mix	Cotton
....	....	....	......	....	....	....
....	....	....	......	....	....	....
....	....	....	......	....	....	....
....	....	....	......	....	....	....
....	....	....	......	....	....	....
....	....	....	......	....	....	....
....	....	....	......	....	....	....
....	....	....	......	....	....	....

II. SALES INFORMATION
2. On which brands have you most volume?

   1st choice.................... Why?...................
   2nd choice.................... Why?...................
   3rd choice.................... Why?...................

3. Which is the most profitable line of blankets to handle?
   .... Why?........................

4. Which, in your opinion, is the best brand or line of blankets on the market?.................. Why?................
   Which is the second best?........... Why?...........

5. To what types of stores or institutions do you sell blankets (in order of importance)?

   (a) .... (d) ....
   (b) .... (e) ....
   (c) .... (f) ....

6. What is the proportion of sales between pair and single blankets?
   Single blankets? ....% Pair blankets? ....%

III. STYLE
7. Of your total woolen blanket sales, what approximate percentage is in—

   (a) White   ....%
   (b) Solid colors   ....%
   (c) Reversible colors ....%
   (d) Plaids   ....%
   (e) Fancies   ....%

8. Which of these types is increasing and which decreasing?

	Increasing	Decreasing
(a) White	....	....
(b) Solid colors	....	....
(c) Reversible colors	....	....
(d) Plaids	....	....
(e) Fancies	....	....

9. Is there a difference in the relative popularity of these types in rural districts that you serve as compared with cities?

Yes .... No ....

What is the approximate percentage of sales in each—

	Rural	Urban	
(a) White	....	....	= 100
(b) Solid colors	....	....	= 100
(c) Reversible colors	....	....	= 100
(d) Plaids	....	....	= 100
(e) Fancies	....	....	= 100

NOTE: Figures for "Rural" and "Urban" must total 100 for each color.

10. Mention and describe any special weaves or constructions that are gaining in popularity?

11. What are the best selling sizes?

	Single Bed		Double Bed	
	1st choice	2nd choice	1st choice	2nd choice
54 x 76	....	....	....	....
60 x 76	....	....	....	....
60 x 80	....	....	....	....
60 x 84	....	....	....	....
64 x 76	....	....	....	....
66 x 80	....	....	....	....
66 x 84	....	....	....	....
66 x 90	....	....	....	....
68 x 80	....	....	....	....
70 x 80	....	....	....	....
72 x 84	....	....	....	....
80 x 90	....	....	....	....

Comment: Have you any complaint, or can you suggest any improvement that can be made in blankets?

Interviewer's Name: ....

Date: ....

City: ....

FIG. 7

A good jobber questionnaire

information which discloses their business affairs and must be shown a good reason for giving any information at all. Technical questions are apt to bring poor answers from jobbers and are often better omitted. A good jobber questionnaire is shown in Fig. 7 on pages 48 and 49.

Data obtained from jobbers portray valuable present facts. If trends are desired, it is best to ask a number of factual questions from which the trends may be calculated, rather than ask for the trends themselves. Jobbers are relatively few in number; so the facts which they give, although of value in themselves, are particularly useful to check against data received from other sources.

4. *Dealers.* Dealers are best approached by personal interview. A mail questionnaire may be substituted when a personal interview is not possible, yet the personal interview commonly yields better information. All of the dealers who handle a product cannot, in most cases, be contacted; therefore care must be taken to cover a representative group, allowance being made for geographical differences, variation in the size of stores, and similar factors. Reports from dealers yield straightforward facts and information about the trend of demand. This latter information is most satisfactorily obtained by asking several factual questions and analyzing the answers.

5. *Consumers.* The nature of the product and the survey will determine whether it is desirable to approach consumers by mail questionnaire or personal interview. In either case, all of the consumers cannot be reached; therefore special care must be taken to get a representative sample of the users. Consumers are commonly classified according to income groups, occupation, age, sex, etc. These classifications should be used in each geographical unit which the survey covers, even though some modifications are necessary, due to local peculiarities.

The facts obtained from consumers are of prime importance. The large number of the reports makes thorough analysis possible. When checked against other sources of current data, reliance can usually be placed upon the ideas of consumers.

6. *Ideal market data.* For ideal market analysis comprehensive data should be collected. Thorough bibliographical work should precede actual field investigation. The investigation should be carried on by personal interviews with experts, jobbers, retailers, and consumers. Mail questionnaires may supplement this work on certain points, so that representative samples of sufficient size may be more easily obtained. Analysis of the returns should be made to check the conclusions of one group against the other. Where discrepancies occur, the reason should be found, regardless of the additional work required. Analysis of the facts should thus make reliable results.

Relation of Field Work to Market Analysis.—The managers of a concern may think that consumers buy a product because it is better or more useful than a competing article. They, however, may not know. Field research tells them why consumers buy any particular article. If the belief of the management is correct, facts now verify it; if wrong, no serious mistake in policy will have been made before the actual facts are learned.

Is it desirable to change the container of a product? Would a smaller and lower-priced package be desirable? Is the advertising appeal correct? An investigation alone can give the answers to such questions. Field research is usually the best way of getting the necessary information.

When business organizations are considering changes of policy, the best judgment obtainable is needed. This calls for actual facts, analysis of them, application of the analysis of the particular problem, and finally, a decision based upon these without emotion and prejudice entering in.

Forecasting is impossible without a knowledge of past and present facts, treated in a statistical manner so as to show trends. Records may give past facts, but field research alone can give those of the immediate present, and these alone can give a sound basis for analysis and judgment. In brief, field research is an absolutely necessary tool in market analysis.

Statistical Approach.—The basis of all market-research work, where a considerable number of people are approached, is statistical. The collected data mean little until they are tabulated and arranged in a logical manner. A few of the principles which are commonly used will now be explained.

NUMBER OF PERSONS INTERVIEWED

Answers	100	150	200	500		
Favorable....	25%	24%	26%	25%		
Unfavorable..	75%	76%	74%	75%		

FIG. 8

Chart showing lack of variation in answers to a question in increasing number of interviews

1. *Sampling.* It may be assumed that a moderately large number of items chosen *at random* from a much larger group, will contain the essential characteristics of the greater group. Sampling is the process of choosing a sufficiently large number of people in each major group which is of interest for the survey. For purposes of comparison, these groups will normally be broken down into smaller ones. It is necessary, therefore, that the number of samples in each subdivision must not be too small.

The illustration given in Fig. 8 indicates that 100 interviews would have been sufficient, yet it is always desirable to have too many rather than too few interviews.

2. *Tabulation.* In the process of tabulation the data obtained through a survey are arranged so that comparable material is placed in convenient tables. These tables may

later be presented in graphic form. For this purpose such answers as "yes" and "no" are most easily tabulated, but many others, such as the comparative importance of various reasons, popularity of brands, etc., are readily dealt with. Unless the question asked of each person is identical, tabulation becomes very difficult or impossible. In unorganized form, the information collected by survey is of little value. Tabulation is necessary before analysis can take place.

3. *Averages*. Averages of numerous kinds are used in the statistical treatment of data. Several kinds will be described.

A. *Simple arithmetic average or mean*. This is obtained by adding up the total of a group of items and dividing by the number of items. For example, the consumption of coffee might be ten pounds per person in one town and sixteen pounds in another town. Adding these two together would give twenty-six. Dividing by two would give thirteen pounds per person as the average for the two towns.

B. *Weighted arithmetic average*. The simple arithmetic average makes no allowance for differences in the value of the various items considered. The weighted average does. For example, in the above case, the first town might have twice the population of the second; therefore it ought to be twice as important in determining the average. If ten (the number of pounds consumed per person in the larger town) were multiplied by two, then sixteen (the number of pounds consumed per person in the smaller town) added, giving thirty-six, and the total divided by three, the sum of the weights, the result would be twelve (see Table 1), the average per capita coffee consumption of the two towns, when weighted according to population. The units from which the average is made can be weighted according to all essential factors, and in this manner the relative importance of all of the items, making up an average, can be allowed for.

TABLE I. ILLUSTRATIONS OF SIMPLE ARITHMETIC AND
WEIGHTED AVERAGES

Town population	Consumption of coffee per person	Simple arithmetic average (pounds per person)	Average weighted according to population (pounds per person)
A 10,000 B 5,000	10 16	$\dfrac{10 + 16}{2} = 13$	$\dfrac{(10 \times 2) + 16}{3} = 12$

To take another example, the question, "What are your three best selling branches of coffee, named in order of volume of sales?" might be asked. First choice might be given a weight of 5, second choice a weight of 3, and third choice a weight of 1. If one hundred grocers answered this question, the tabulation would follow the procedure shown below:

Brand A

50 (first choice)   × 5 (weight for first choice)   = 250
30 (second choice) × 3 (weight for second choice) = 90
20 (third choice) × 1 (weight for third choice) = 20
                                                    ───
                                                    360

The weighted total for Brand A would be 360, which, when divided by the 100 observations, gives a weighted average of 3.6 for Brand A. Brands B, C, D, etc., would have weighted averages calculated in the same manner, and a comparison of these would give the proper significance to each item as regards volume of sales.

C. *Mode.* The mode is the point of greatest frequency in any series. A survey might show that the average age of the purchasers of a product was thirty-two years. Arranging the age groups in order from ten to sixty, however, might show that the number of purchasers between ten and twenty years of age was negligible, that the number of purchasers of the age of twenty-five years was very great, and that there was a scattered group of purchasers above thirty years of age. The point of greatest frequency, twenty-five years, is of much more importance than the mathematical mean of thirty-two years. In some series, more than one mode may exist. For example, a series of prices might show a definite concentration in three price classes. The following series indicate the occurrence of single and multiple modes.

TABLE 2. ILLUSTRATIONS OF MODE AND MEDIAN

Series	Frequency	Series	Frequency
5	2	$1.00	4
6	1	1.50	10◄Mode
7	2	2.00	2
8	8◄Mode	2.50	3
9	3◄Median	3.00	11◄Mode
10	2	3.50	5◄Median
11	1	4.00	2
12	1	4.50	1
13	2	5.00	10◄Mode
14	1	5.50	3
		6.00	1

D. *Median.* Where any group of statistics has been "arranged"—that is, set in progressive order, the median represents the exact middle item, if the total number of items are odd; or if the number of items is even, the median lies between the two middle items. The median is illustrated in Table 2. The median and mode do not coincide in the illustrations, although in some cases this occurs.

MARKET-ANALYSIS PROCEDURE

TOPICAL OUTLINE

1. Product
   History
   Physical characteristics
   Product policies
   Economic status
   Who buys?
   Patent situation
   Substitutes
   Package

2. Company
   History
   Organization
   Records
      purchasing
      production
      sales
   Plant

3. Industry
   Production
      by volume
      by value
      by investment
      by workers
   Labor situation
   Economic trends
   Relation to other in-
      dustries
   Geographical grouping
   Integration
   Combination
   Foreign situation

4. Competition
   Monopoly-character
   Bases
      price
      size of companies
      number of companies
      location
      line of goods
      service
      labor
      transportation
      trend
      good will
      personality
      patent
      cost of overcoming
      foreign competition
      combine with a com-
         petitor?

5. Customers
   Why do they buy from
      company?
   How classify?
   Former customers
      why lost?
      chances of recovering

6. Ultimate consumer
   Why is product bought?
   Sex
   Race
   Religion
   Age
   Disabilities
   Prejudices
   Buying habits
   Occupation
   Class
   Expert knowledge
   Literacy

7. Market—nature and size
  Complexity
  Geographical extent
   Grouped or scattered
  Urban or rural
  Population
  Indices of market
  Interdependent markets

8. Market—potentiality and
   limitations
  Opportunities
  Original and replacement
  Limitations
   price
   fashion
   cost of operation
   seasonal
   climate and weather
   second-hand situation
   government restrictions
   business cycle

9. Distribution
  Trends as to functions
  Effect of
   product
   service
   financing
   volume of business
   market
   credit
   channels
     direct or indirect
     possible links
   jobbers and dealers

10. Sales
  Character of sales force
  Sales policies
   jobbers and dealers
   terms and discounts
  Sales tests
  Repeat sales

11. Advertising
  Purpose
  Scope
  Advertising done
  Appeals
  How directed?
  Media
  Tests

FIG. 9
An outline of market-analysis procedure

CHAPTER V

PROCESSES OF RESEARCH

THE scientific method is the same, whether applied to physics, biology, geology, business, or advertising. It begins with the gathering of facts, continues with the registration and measurement of the data thus obtained, and then arranges, charts, and tabulates this information. Finally, tentative conclusions are drawn. When these have been tested and reduced to a workable hypothesis, they are generally termed "principles" or "laws." In applied sciences, such as medicine, advertising, and business, such conclusions are not so exact as in the case of mathematics. Nevertheless, they are unquestionably of great use in determining policies. The methods used are the same in all types of research, and scientific procedure may be divided into four processes:

1. Observation
2. Analysis and comparison
3. Generalization
4. Verification

Field research employs these four processes in the following manner:

1. *Observation.* The collecting of facts is carried on by observation of various kinds. Personal interviews, telephone interviews, group interviews, mail questionnaires, and bibliographical sources are used for gathering the facts.

From whatever sources the data are secured, there are ten properties which they should have. These are:

a. *Accuracy* is the base of all observation. This requires a search for the real, underlying facts as well as an accurate recording of them.

b. *Reliability* of data is also a fundamental requirement. The ordinary rule is to procure data as close to the original source as possible. The information obtained and the sources from which it is taken must be of a nature which can be verified.

c. *Impartiality* must be absolute in presenting data. Questions must be so worded as to give no clue to the desired answer. No guiding of results in any way is permissible.

d. *Applicability* of facts gathered to the problem in hand is necessary. There should be no gathering of data merely for the sake of doing so. All data should be pertinent to the specific case.

e. *Availability* of data obtained is important. The observations should be recorded in such form that they will prove intelligible for purposes of analysis and comparison.

f. *Comprehensiveness* demands that all necessary data bearing on the subject be gathered. The omission of one factor may overbalance the results.

g. *Representativeness* requires that the observations gathered should be fully indicative of conditions in the whole field. Sufficient data from each group investigated must be secured to make the results representative.

h. *Judgment* in weighing, assorting, and evaluating the information obtained in the interviews is essential. No pertinent fact should be omitted, no extraneous fact included, when formulating a judgment.

i. *System* is needed to make observations quickly, thoroughly, and at a minimum expense.

j. *Control* of observations should be exercised in so far as possible. That is, care must be taken to see that observations made in a given case will produce results. Decisions must be made as to the number of observations required and under what conditions they shall be made. Control is essential to the success of any organized survey.

2. *Analysis and comparison.* As the information comes in from the field, it is first edited to make sure it is in

correct form. The material is then turned over to a statistician or statistical department, where it is arranged in such manner that it can be easily understood and readily compared.

The proper tabulation and correlation of information which has been collected are vital to the successful completion of an investigation. While some studies are so simple that a novice might tabulate the results, most investigations bring to light a complex mass of valuable information which can be classified only through the intelligent use of mathematical processes. This work should be done by experts in the home office.

A general outline of this procedure is:

a. *Editing.* Before any tabulation can be done, it is important to edit observations carefully for inaccuracy, bias, incompleteness, or other factors which would be likely to prejudice the validity of the statistical compilation.

b. *Tabulation.* Observations are recorded as they come in on a tabulation schedule or recapitulation sheet. This is made up, either in advance of the actual receipt of the observations, where the type of answer is known, or as the answers come in.

c. *Classification.* A number of classifications is usually possible, such as geographic distribution, age, sex, volume of business, or preferences expressed. Classification may be made from basic records on the tabulation schedule, or results may be recapitulated later on special sheets.

d. *Computation and comparison.* The next step is to compare data in order to bring out relationships. It may be necessary to make certain computations at this point to reduce different sets of statistics to a comparable basis.

e. *Correlation.* It is desirable, if possible, to establish some relation between a specific set of statistics and the market. If a direct relation can be found, this is known as a "market index."

UNITED STATES DEPARTMENT OF COMMERCE
BUREAU OF FOREIGN AND DOMESTIC COMMERCE

SURVEY OF CURRENT BUSINESS
WEEKLY SUPPLEMENT

WASHINGTON, D. C., DECEMBER 4, 1930

WEEKLY BUSINESS INDICATORS

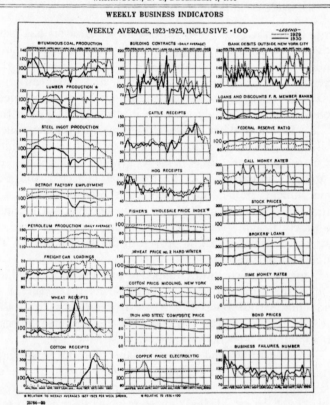

FIG. 10

These complicated facts are made intelligible by the use of indices
and graphs

f. *Graphic interpretation.* Whenever statistical tabulations can be reduced to simple forms, then they may be graphed or charted to show relationships more clearly. The graph is a method of presentation which is of great importance in all market and advertising research because of the greater clarity and ease with which generalizations may be made from these pictorial forms.

3. *Generalization.* When the work of analysis has been properly done, the drawing of conclusions is greatly simplified. It is, however, invariably a task calling for the exercise of the keenest discrimination and judgment.

To formulate answers to definite questions of business policy requires not only accurate information, but also the ability to know what to do with that information. Such ability is gained only through long and active experience in marketing work. Bias must be avoided at all costs, yet a great familiarity with the material collected and the environment from which it comes is essential. Not only must the generalization or conclusion be true, but it must be practical and specific. The reasoning must be clear so that the conclusion can be proved to the satisfaction of all interested parties.

Logic is of two kinds, inductive and deductive. Induction is the formulation of a principle as the result of a wide number of observations. It is reasoning from the specific to the general. Deduction is the converse process of applying a general principle to a specific case.

Both induction and deduction are used in marketing research. A wide number of observations must be made, the resultant data must be compared, and general principles must be established. These principles are to be used as practical business policies, subject to modification as individual conditions may require. The process of generalization is probably the most difficult task in field research, owing to the complexity of conditions and their geographical variation.

4. *Verification.* To corroborate or to disprove findings requires not only a knowledge of technical processes which have been used, but also of logic. Testing has a technique of its own.

The conclusions of a research survey cannot be considered final until they have been given a thorough trial. If interviews have been used for the basic data, mail questionnaires may be used to check the results. If the data have come from consumers, a few interviews with dealers may help to corroborate this evidence. Experts may be consulted in any of these cases. When possible, it is also desirable to apply the results over a small area at first, using what might be called test application. Such methods lead to the final adoption of policies which are as valid as present technique can accomplish.

Application of Results.—In both generalization and verification, the guiding principle must be practicability. The easiest sure generalization may be that a new style of product is desirable, a new container is needed, or a change in the method of compensating salesmen is essential. These answers are too vague. The specific new product which is desirable, the best possible container, and a fully-worked-out improved method of compensating salesmen should be given. Every condition in the industry and the company must be taken into consideration in making these recommendations. An ideal new product from the production viewpoint may be impossible from the marketing angle because an entirely new set of outlets might have to be developed. Each factor must be considered in relation to all others.

CHAPTER VI

MARKET RESEARCH AND ITS PRACTICE

THE outline of market research which is given here is a practical one from the viewpoint of actually conducting surveys. The succeeding chapters develop the main points in this:

1. Exposition, in writing, of the scope and purpose of the work.
2. Selection of the executive who is responsible for the survey and the choice of his assistants with their respective responsibilities.
3. Creation of an analysis outline.
4. Internal situation survey, or situation study, which utilizes all of the company's available records.
5. Bibliographical work. (Sufficient investigation is made at this time to ascertain just what is available and how up-to-date this is.)
6. Written agreement upon what essential facts can be obtained only through field work, thus specifically listing the field work to be done.
7. Decision as to the methods in the field work, the choice lying between the following methods or some combination of them.
   a. Personal interview.
   b. Mail questionnaire.
   c. Telephone interview.
   d. Group interview.
   e. Field test.
8. Selection of the representative part of the market to be covered in the field work; classification of consumers, and the like.

Bissell & Land
INCORPORATED
Advertising and Merchandising
339 Boulevard of the Allies
Pittsburgh

Date of Interview _____

Name of Investigator _____

Number of Interview _____

Edited by _____

Consumer Field Survey

Lifting Jacks

1. Name of Concern:
_____

2. Address:
No. _____ Street _____
City _____ State _____

3. Individual Interviewed:
Name _____
Official Position _____

4. Industrial Classification:
Public Utilities _____ 5—0
  Government Depts. _____ 1
  Electric R. R. and Bus Lines _____ 2
  Telephone and Telegraph _____ 3
  Gas, Water and Electric _____ 4
Industrial _____ 5
  Mills and Factories _____ 6
  Oil Producers and Refiners _____ 7
  Car and Locomotive Builders _____ 8
Mining and Lumbering _____ 9
  Coal _____ 5—0
  Ore _____ 1
  Quarries _____ 2
  Logging and Lumbering Co's. _____ 3
Contractors and Builders _____ 4
  Building and Construction _____ 5
  Sewer and Water _____ 6
  Wrecking and Moving _____ 7

5. What uses do you make of Jacks? 7 & 8
_____

6. What is your greatest Jack problem? 9—
_____

7. What makes of Jacks are you now using?
( ) Buckeye _____ 10—1

( ) Duff _____ 2
( ) Joyce _____ 3
( ) Norton _____ 4
( ) Simplex _____ 5
( ) Other (give name) _____ 6

8. Why do you prefer this particular make over others?
( ) Cheaper _____ 11—1
( ) Easier operation _____ 2
( ) Greater durability _____ 3
( ) Lighter in weight _____ 4
( ) Previous satisfactory experience with same product _____ 5
( ) Greater lifting power compared to rating _____ 6
( ) Other reasons (explain) _____ 7

9. What sizes of ratchet jacks do you use 12 & 13 and how many of each size?
Size in tons   No. used

10. What sizes of screw jacks do you use 14 & 15 and how many of each size?
Size in tons   No. used

11. How many Jacks do you buy each year?
Ratchet Jacks _____ 16—
Screw Jacks _____ 17—

12. How long do Jacks last in your type of work?
Ratchet Jacks _____ 18—
Screw Jacks _____ 19—

13. Do you buy:
( ) Direct from manufacturer _____ 20—1
( ) From jobber _____ 2
( ) From retailer _____ 3

14. Do you use any of the following special purpose Jacks? If so, how many of each? Number
( ) Pushing and pulling _____ 21—1
( ) Traversing bases _____ 2
( ) Oil well jacks _____ 3
( ) Cable reel jacks _____ 4
( ) Pole jacks _____ 5
( ) Armature lifts _____ 6
( ) Trench Braces _____ 7
( ) Pinion pullers _____ 8

15. What influenced you most to begin using your present make of Jacks?
_____ 22—

16. Which one of the following would influence you most to use another make of Jacks?
( ) Advertising _____ 23—1
( ) Greater factor of safety _____ 2
( ) Honest rating of lifting capacity _____ 3
( ) Lower first cost _____ 4
( ) Lower ultimate cost _____ 5
( ) Personal visit of a salesman _____ 6
( ) Recommendation of your dealer or supplier _____ 7
( ) Recommendation of friends _____ 8
( ) Reputation of manufacturer _____ 9

17. In what order do you place the following attributes when you buy Jacks? 24 & 25
(First choice, No. 1; Second, No. 2, etc.)
( ) Durability
( ) Ease of operation
( ) Ease of securing repair parts

FIG. 11

The first page of a precoded dealer questionnaire which is not
meant to be memorized but to be filled in during the interview

9. Formulation and testing of questionnaires.
10. Accomplishment of field work and completion of bibliographical work.
11. Editing and tabulating the returns.

Interviewer [1]...........   HOME

Date ....   A [5-0] ....
                                    B [5-1] ....
City [2] ....   C [5-2] ....
Zone [3 & 4]..............   D [5-3] ....

1. No. in family [6 & 7].................................

2. Do you own? [8-0]...........
        rent? [8-1]...........

3. Family head's occupation [9 & 10]..............

4. Car, make [11&12]........Year [13&14]......

5. Radio Yes [15-0].........Battery [16-0].......
         No [15-1].........Elec.   [16-1].......

6. Automatic Refrigerator? Yes [17-0]...........
                           No [17-1]...........

FIG. 12

A page from a consumer questionnaire made to fit into a small
loose-leaf notebook

12. Analysis of data, using the statistical method when possible, and drawing conclusions.
13. Testing the conclusions.
14. Writing the report.
15. Presenting the conclusions.

Types of Field Work.—The steps used in ordinary
field-research procedure which require detailed treatment

are handled in other chapters; so reference will be made here only to the relative merits of the different types of field or survey methods.

The Personal Interview.—This is a well-recognized method of gathering business facts (see questionnaires in

---

8. At what type of store do you buy toilet tissue?

	Chain	Ind.
Drug	(10-0)	(10-4)
Grocery	(10-1)	(10-5)
Hardware	(10-2)	(10-6)
Department	(10-3)	(10-7)

9. How much do you usually pay per roll? (11 & 12)
. . . .

10. Do you buy it by brand? Yes (13-0). . . . .
                            No (13-1). . . . .

11. If so, what brand? (14 & 15). . . . .

12. Why do you buy this brand? (16 & 17). . . . .
. . . .

13. If you do not buy by brand, why not? (18 & 19)
. . . .

Fig. 13
A personal-interview questionnaire

Figs. 11, 12, 13, 14, 15, 16, etc., on pages 65, 66, 67, 68, 69, 70, etc.). Certain types of information can be obtained in no other way. *Standards of Research*, published in 1929 by the Meredith Publishing Company under the direction of Jean F. Carroll, lists the following advantages and disadvantages of the personal interview:

Advantages of personal interview:

1. Only way to secure information where discussion is necessary.

WOOLEN BLANKET SURVEY

CONSUMER QUESTIONNAIRE

1. How many, and what makes of blankets have you?

No.	Brands	(Check 1) Wool	(Check 1) Cotton Mix	Cotton	(Check 1) Single	(Check 1) Pair
1	North Star	14-1	14-2	14-3	14-1	14-5
2	Esmond	15-1	15-2	15-3	15-4	15-5
3	Kenwood	16-1	16-2	16-3	16-4	16-5
4	St. Mary's	17-1	17-2	17-3	17-4	17-5
5	Nashua	18-1	18-2	18-3	18-4	18-5
6	Chatham	19-1	19-2	19-3	19-4	19-5
7	Old Town	20-1	20-2	20-3	20-4	20-5
8	Mariposa	21-1	21-2	21-3	21-4	21-5
9	Lady Seymour	22-1	22-2	22-3	22-4	22-5
10	Pendleton	23-1	23-2	23-3	23-4	23-5
11	Oregon City	24-1	24-2	24-3	24-4	24-5
12	Don't know	25-1	25-2	25-3	25-4	25-5
13	All others	26-1	26-2	26-3	26-4	26-5

2. How many blankets (white) have you?   27

How many colored blankets have you?   28

How many reversible blankets have you?   29

How many comforters have you?   30

How many quilts have you?   31

How many throws have you?   32

3. How many beds have you?   Total: 33

Beds

Single 34-1   Three-quarter 34-2   Double 34-3

4. Do you vary the weight of blankets according to seasons by using:

    1. Different weight of blankets 35-1

            or

    2. By varying the number of blankets 35-2

Fig. 14

First page of a complicated and precoded consumer questionnaire. The interviewer is not expected to memorize such a questionnaire, but is directed to fill it as the information is received

E. A. Moffatt
Feed Mill Research
City Club Bldg., St. Louis, Mo.

DEALER INVESTIGATION

Date....................................

A. IDENTIFICATION:

1. State....................................

2. Town....................................

3. Population of town....................................
   Population of county....................................

4. Name of firm....................................
   ....

5. Rating of firm in Dun's....................................

6. Position of individual interviewed:
   Proprietor....................................
   Manager....................................
   Salesman....................................

7. Kind of store:
   Feed store....................................
   General store....................................
   Co-operative or Company store....................................
   Grocery store....................................

8. Number of stores handling feeds....................................

9. Apparent class of trade:
   High-class trade....................................
   Middle-class trade....................................
   Low-class trade....................................

10. Does dealer do credit business: Yes........ No........

11. Does dealer solicit business: Yes........ No........

12. If yes, how does he do this:
    By personal call....................................
    By personal call with
        feed manufacturer's salesman....................................
    By telephone....................................

13. Does dealer advertise: Yes........ No........

14. If yes, how does he advertise:
    Display space in local paper....................................
    Reading items in local paper....................................
    Distributes hand bills....................................
    Card in telephone or city directory....................................
    Form letters or circulars....................................
    Movie slides....................................
    Theatre programs or curtains....................................
    Street car cards....................................
    Country road, farm or fence signs....................................
    Painted signs on barns, fences, etc....................................
    Novelty advertising....................................

B. SALES INFORMATION:

1. Do you carry in stock feed from more than one feed mill
   at a time: Yes............... No...............
   How many mills....................................
   Why....................................

2. What mills have you dealt with the past year:
   ....
   ....
   ....
   Why....................................

3. What mill or mills are you doing business with now:
   ....
   ....
   Why....................................
   Where do shipments come from?....................................
   ....

4. What brands of feeds are you selling now:
   Horse or Mule Feed....................................
   Dairy feed 24%....................................
   Dairy Feed 20%....................................
   Dairy Feed 16%....................................
   Poultry Feed:
       Starting Feed....................................
       Chick Feed....................................
       Growing Mash....................................
       Starting and Growing Mash....................................
       Developer....................................
       Eggmash....................................
       Fattener....................................
       Allmash....................................
   Hog Feed....................................

5. How much feed do you sell:

	Carloads per Year	Carloads per Month	Sacks per Year	Sacks per Month	Volume is Increasing	Decreasing
Horse or Mule Feed						
Dairy Feed						
Poultry Feed						
Hog Feed						

6. What is the strongest or best selling brand in your territory:
   Horse or Mule Feed....................................
   Dairy   Feed....................................
   Poultry Feed....................................
   Hog   Feed....................................

7. What other local dealer is your hardest competitor:
   ....

8. What brands of feed is he selling:
   Horse or Mule Feed....................................
   Dairy   Feed....................................
   Poultry Feed....................................
   Hog   Feed....................................

(over)

FIG. 15

Part A of this dealer questionnaire illustrates the minute classification of respondents which is sometimes necessary

2. Investigators may obtain additional valuable information not contemplated when questions were planned.
3. Hard to secure extensive "opinions" by other methods.
4. Easy to visit enough proper stores or consumers to secure an adequate sample.

Date ....

Interviewer ....

1. What brand of cigarette do you smoke?
   Ans. ....
2. Why do you prefer it?
   Ans. ....
3. What suggestions have you to make as to improving cigarettes?
   Ans. ....
4. What do you think of the new Camel package?
   Ans. ....
   ....
5. What might be done to improve it?
   Ans. ....
   ....
6. To what extent is smoking among women a fad?
   Ans. ....

Fig. 16

A simple and factual consumer questionnaire. Unskilled investigators might be used with this questionnaire

5. Excellent method for very limited investigations.
6. Good way to test questionnaires to be sent by mail.

Disadvantages of personal interview:
1. Requires long time to cover extensive territory.
2. Extensive investigations requiring large corps of field men are frequently adversely affected by:
   a. Failure of all men to secure information uniformly.

b. Inability of some of the field men.
3. Large expense if extensive territory is to be covered.
4. Hard to select small territory which is true sample of larger territory.
5. Possible dishonesty of investigators which is extremely hard to detect in large investigations.
6. Field investigators may be biased by their own reaction to the problem, by their education, and by their particular moods during the interviews.

The main advantages obtained through the use of personal interviews are securing samples of the market under controlled conditions and gaining information in addition to brief answers to the question asked. This additional information is of prime importance because the preliminary investigation may fail to indicate the need of certain data which may later prove essential. In many instances concerns have found that the facts which were not deliberately sought were of more importance than those for which the survey was made.

The main disadvantage of using the personal interview method is that it is considered to be more expensive than the other common means for determining market facts. This is necessarily true only in the case of a traveling field force, as will be shown later.

The Mail Questionnaire.—The mail questionnaire has the following advantages and disadvantages:[1]

Advantages of mail questionnaire:
1. Information can be secured from people at distant points at low expense.
2. The range of territory to be covered is limited only by the limits of mail service.
3. It is possible to reach people who cannot be reached by any other method.

[1] *Standards of Research*, by Jean F. Carroll. Meredith Publishing Company, 1929.

Cosmetic Needs and Habits

1—Can you describe your *type* of skin?..   Yes ( ) No ( )

2—   What type is it?..   ....

3—   Which of these general descriptions applies to your skin? (Circle number)
        1—Dry   *3*—Average
        2—Oily   *4*—Generally dry but oily in places

4—   Is your skin "fine" and sensitive, or of normal quality?................................   Fine ( ) Norm. ( )

5—Which of these skin *problems* have you experienced? (Circle numbers)
        1—Large pores   *5*—Dullness
        2—Blackheads   *6*—Scaly condition
        3—Wrinkles or lines   *7*—Coarse texture
        4—Sallowness   *8*—Blotchy appearance

6—When do you cleanse your skin or give it special care? (Circle numbers and describe)
    Just what do you do and what preparations do you use?
        1—In morning, on rising..
        2—Before noon meal..
        3—Before going out..
        4—Before evening meal...
        5—Before going to bed...

7—   Which of these occasions is most important? (Circle number).................................   1 2 3 4 5

8—   Why?..

9—Do you use *cold cream* or *cleansing* cream to cleanse your skin?........   Yes ( ) No ( )

10—   What kind?...

11—   Is it satisfactory or unsatisfactory?.....................................   Sat. ( ) Uns. ( )

12—   Why?..

13—   How long have you been using a cream of this sort?..........................Years

14—   If price were no object which kind would you use?..........................

15—Do you use any *nourishing* or *softening cream?*...........................   Yes ( ) No ( )

16—   What kind?...

17—   Is it satisfactory or unsatisfactory?.....................................   Sat. ( ) Uns. ( )

18—   Why?..

19—   What does it do for the skin?...
    ....

20—   How long have you been using a cream of this sort?..........................Years

21—   If price were no object which kind would you use?..........................

22—Do you use *vanishing* cream or any *other powder base?*.................   Yes ( ) No ( )

29—   What kind?...

30—   Is it satisfactory or unsatisfactory?.....................................   Sat. ( ) Uns. ( )

31—   Why?..

32— How long have you been using a cream of this sort?...Years

33— If price were no object which kind would you use?...

34—Do you feel that the higher priced creams are better and more reliable?....   Yes ( ) No ( )

35—Which do you believe is the chief reason for the high price of expensive creams?

....

36—If both sold at the same price which would you prefer—what you now use
or a salon product such as Elizabeth Arden or Dorothy Gray?..............   Salon( ).Own ( )

37—Do you feel that a cream must be expensive in order to be really good?...   Yes ( ) No ( )

38—Do you use any *facial liquid* on your skin?...   Yes ( ) No ( )

39— What kind?...

40— At what time of day do you use it?...

41— Do you use it alone or with other preparations?...   Alone( )Other( )

42— With what preparations?...

43— Do you use it *after* or *before* other preparations?...   After ( ) Befr ( )

44— How long have you been using a facial liquid?...Years

45—Do you use *soap and water* on your face?.......................................   Yes ( ) No ( )

46— What kind?...

47— How often?...

48— Does it have an undesirable effect?...   Yes ( ) No ( )

49— What effect does it have?...

FACTS ABOUT AMBRŌSIA

50—What was your reason for deciding to try Ambrosia?...

51—When do you use it? (Circle numbers)

    1—In morning, on rising   *4*—Before evening meal
    2—Before noon meal   *5*—Before going to bed
    3—Before going out

52—How do you use Ambrosia? (Circle number)

    1—Alone   *3*—Before cream
    2—After cream   *4*—After washing face with soap

53—How do you apply Ambrosia? (Circle number)

    1—With absorbent cotton   *4*—With Kleenex
    2—With hand towel   *5*—With gauze
    3—With bath towel   *6*—With cloth or wash rag

54—After using Ambrosia do you Pat dry, Wipe off, or Rinse off?...............   P( )W( )R( )

55—Are you substituting Ambrosia for a cleansing method you were using or
using it in addition to your regular cleansing methods?.......................   Sub.( )Add.( )

56—How long have you been using Ambrosia?...Months

57—Have you noticed any change in your skin during that time?.................   Yes ( ) No ( )

58—   What change?.............

59—How much of the sample used? Less than half, More than half, or All?..   L( )M( )All( )

60—What is your frank opinion of it?.............

61—Is it a satisfactory powder base?.............   Yes ( ) No ( )

62—   Reason.............

63—Describe the sensation when you used it. Pleasant or Unpleasant?..........   Pl.( )Unpl.( )

63A—   Reason.....,

64—Describe the odor. Pleasant or Unpleasant?.............   Pl.( )Unpl.( )

64A—   Reason.............

65—Is it used by the man of the house?.............   Yes ( ) No ( )

66—   Does he Like it or Dislike it?.............   Like( )Dis.( )

67—   How does he use it? After shaving or as a cleanser?.............   Shav.( )Clen.( )

67A—   Remarks.............

68—Have you purchased Ambrosia?.............   Yes ( ) No ( )

69—Do you intend to?.............   Yes ( ) No ( )

69A—   Reason.............

70—When would it give best results, in winter or summer?.............   Wint.( )Sum.( )

71—   Why?.............

Story on Care of the Hands

72—What do you use in the care of your hands? (Circle number and give name of product)

   1—Hand lotion.............

   2—Vanishing cream.............

   3—Cold cream.............

   4—Other type of product.............

73—   Does your husband use it for his hands?.............   Yes ( ) No ( )

74—   Do you use it on your children's Hands or Face? (Check, if used).............   H ( ) F ( )

75—When do you have the *greatest need* for a preparation to use on your hands? (Circle uses mentioned as most important)

1—After household work	6—After washing clothes
2—After office work	7—After using soap
3—After dishwashing	8—After exposure to cold
4—After gardening	9—After sunburn
5—After driving car	10—After windburn

FIG. 17

A personal-interview questionnaire which illustrates the need for a minute classification of respondents

4. It is usually less expensive than other methods.

5. People can fill out questionnaires at a convenient time.

Disadvantages of mail questionnaire:

1. It is difficult to secure replies from a very large number of those who receive the questionnaire.

2. The questions may not be properly or accurately filled out.

3. It is not always possible to determine whether the people returning questionnaires are representative of all to whom the questionnaires were sent.

4. Only information directly requested is likely to be given.

The main advantage of using the mail questionnaire lies in the fact that it is often the most economical method of obtaining the facts. On the other hand, you cannot tell who will answer the questionnaire and so do not know whether the result will be a representative sample of those to whom it was sent. (Examples of mail questionnaires are given in Figs. 19, 20, 21, 22, 23 on pages 77, 78, 79, 80 and 81, etc.)

Personal Interview vs. Mail Questionnaire.—The personal interview is commonly considered more expensive than the mail questionnaire. This is not necessarily true in all cases. A comparison of the personal interview and the mail questionnaire involves other considerations, however, and these will be discussed first.

Validity of Samples.—When personal interviews are used, it is not difficult to spread the completed questionnaires among geographic areas, income groups, residential areas, and the like. Once the desired divisions are decided upon, the distribution of the interviews is merely an ordinary administrative problem.

In the case of mail questionnaires, no method has yet been devised whereby persons in certain desired groups can be made to respond to the exclusion of other groups. The mailing list can appear ideal, yet the answers may not

CONSUMER QUESTIONNAIRE

Person Interviewed ....

Address .... City ....

1. What brands of insulating materials have you used?
2. For what type of work have you used each brand?
3. Why did you choose each brand for the particular work in question?

Brand Used	Type Work	Reasons for Choosing				
		Ad. Ch.	Contr.	Friend	Exp.	Other

4. What is your opinion of....................?

Favorable .... Unfavorable ....

Neutral .... No answer ....

Points in favor   *Unfavorable*

FIG. 18

Personal-interview questionnaire which shows the value
of comments

CHICAGO   NEW YORK

THE CAPLES COMPANY
452 LEXINGTON AVENUE
(3002 Grand Central Terminal)
NEW YORK CITY

        I will appreciate your assistance in gathering
some information which is very important to one of my
clients.

        The favor I am asking will take only a moment
of your time, and if you will fill out the form below
and put it in the mail, it will be of great assistance to
me in this work. The envelope is stamped and addressed.
It is not necessary to sign your name.

        1. With from $200. to $400. to spend for a two
            or three weeks' vacation, what would your
            several choices be - in order of preference?

            Summer Vacation   Winter Vacation
            1_____   1_____
            2_____   2_____
            3_____   3_____

        2. Have you ever considered a Caribbean Cruise as
            a vacation possibility?

            Summer Vacation   Winter Vacation

            _____   _____

            Why?_____   _____

        3. If you have not, why?
            Summer Vacation   Winter Vacation

            _____   _____

                    Yours very truly,

FIG. 19

A mail questionnaire which frankly asks a favor. It is always
desirable to get both the questionnaire and the accompanying
letter on one sheet

J. WALTER THOMPSON COMPANY
Chicago

410 N. MICHIGAN AVENUE

Dear Madam:

You probably remember having done small favors for people which
they appreciated very much yet which caused you very little trouble.
It is such a favor we are writing to ask of you.

We want to find out what brands of butter and eggs are best known
and most highly regarded by the housekeepers of America.

Won't you please list below all the brands of butter that you are
familiar with in order of your choice?

    1st choice   _____

    2nd   "   _____

    3rd   "   _____

    4th   "   _____

    Other brands _____

Please list below all the brands of eggs that you are familiar with
in order of your choice:

    1st choice   _____

    2nd   "   _____

    3rd   "   _____

    4th   "   _____

    Other brands _____

A Business Reply Envelope which requires no postage is enclosed for
your convenience in returning this to us.

We indeed appreciate your help.

                        Sincerely,

                        J. WALTER THOMPSON COMPANY.

NEW YORK   CHICAGO   BOSTON   CINCINNATI   SAN FRANCISCO   LONDON

FIG. 20

A mail questionnaire which asks for simple but important information. The brevity is commendable

show the desired concentration and dispersion. In addition, there may be no way to check the actual distribution of

QUESTIONNAIRE

(To be filled out by an unmarried woman of the household)

City and State INDIANAPOLIS, INDIANA

1. What make of watch do you own?

   Wrist Elgin (Name of maker) Pocket .... (Name of maker)

2. How long have you had it? 10 yrs.

3. Was it a gift or did you buy it?

   Gift [✓] Bought Myself [ ] (Please check)

4. If you were buying a watch of any kind for yourself now, what make would you select?

   Elgin (Name of maker)

5. Why would you prefer this make of watch? (Please state briefly)

   Keeps good time, very little expense for repairs neat in appearance

6. If you were buying a watch for a man, what make and type would you get?

   Wrist .... (State make) Pocket Elgin (State make)

7. Why? Same reasons as above (Please state briefly)

8. A. My own occupation is Insurance Clerk + Acct or Home Girl [ ] (Please check)

   B. The occupation of my father (or male head of the family) is Retired

9. My family owns a Oldsmobile (Make of car) automobile. formerly Justice of the Peace

FIG. 21

A mail questionnaire as it was received from a respondent

the returns. Information on this subject is scarce, but the example which follows is interesting:

The Procter & Gamble Company[1] compiled a questionnaire and sent it to a large number of persons. The

[1] Editorial, *Printers' Ink*, July 21, 1927.

PUBLIC REACTION BALLOT

General Motors

1. Listed below are some of the factors that cause one <u>dealer</u>
    to be preferred above others. Fill in the blank lines with
    additional factors that influence you.

Then in the square after the factor that counts most with you, write
the figure 10, and in the other squares, write numbers to indicate how each
factor compares in importance to the one you have marked 10. For example:
If personality is the most important factor in choosing a dealer, you would
place 10 in the square after that word. If the attractiveness of his place
of business had about half as much influence with you, put a 5 after that
item, and so on.

PERSONALITY ☐   DEALER'S ADVERTISING ☐

ATTRACTIVENESS OF SHOWROOM ☐   PERSONAL FRIENDSHIP ☐

LOCATION OF SHOWROOM ☐   GIVES A GOOD "DEAL" ☐

GOOD SERVICE ☐   _____ ☐

_____ ☐   _____ ☐

2. The following are some of the reasons for selecting a given
    <u>car</u> in preference to others in its price-class. Fill in
    the blank lines with other factors that influence you.

Then write 10 after the one most important to you, and mark the others
with numbers indicating the relative importance as compared to the one that
was foremost in respect to the influence it has with you.

BODY LINES ☐   DURABILITY ☐

RADIATOR DESIGN ☐   MECHANICAL FEATURES ☐

COLOR ☐   SPEED ☐

GENERAL APPEARANCE ☐   PICK-UP ☐

OPERATING ECONOMY ☐   COMFORT ☐

_____ ☐   _____ ☐

FIG. 22

A mail questionnaire which elicited answers requiring a
preference tabulation

company then proceeded to check up on the results by the following methods:

DEALER MAIL QUESTIONNAIRE
Do not sign your name

1. What makes of lawn mowers do you handle?

   . . . .

   . . . .

2. Which is the best seller? . . . .
   Why? . . . .

3. Is there any demand on the part of your customers for power-driven mowers?

   Electric   Yes . . . .

   No. . . . .

   Gasoline Yes . . . .

   No. . . . .
   (Please check)

4. What complaints do you get on lawn mowers?

5. What suggestions would you offer for improving the present lawn mowers on the market?

6. Could the present manufacturer-jobber policies be improved? . . . . How? . . . .

7. Remarks:

Please return to Percival White, Inc. in the enclosed stamped envelope.

FIG. 23
A mail questionnaire sent to dealers. The questions are simple and direct

1. Copies of the names and addresses of all the persons to whom the mail questionnaire was sent, were kept.

2. Three of the cities thus covered were selected for the purpose of study.

3. Personal interviews were secured with those who had answered the mail questionnaire, and what they said in the interview was compared to the mail questionnaire answers.

4. Personal interviews were secured with those who failed to answer the mail questionnaire, in an attempt to discover what kind of people did not respond. These were conducted very carefully.

5. Personal interviews with those who answered the mail questionnaire were so worded that the housewife did not suspect that the accuracy of her answers by mail were being doubted.

The more significant results of this investigation were:

1. Of the housewives who answered the mail questionnaire, 92 per cent were found to be users of the product and 8 per cent were non-users.

2. Of those who did not answer, 40 per cent were found to be users and 60 per cent were found to be non-users.

3. Those who did answer the mail questionnaire gave information that was exceptionally accurate; only 15 per cent of the answers given in the mail questionnaire differed from those received in the personal interview.

The experience of the Procter & Gamble Company indicates that users of a product are more likely to answer a mail questionnaire than non-users and that the statements given on mail questionnaires have a high degree of dependability. As more studies of this nature become available, the usefulness of the mail questionnaire will increase because its limitations will be better defined.

Type of Information Wanted.—Simple "yes" and "no" questions may receive equally satisfactory answers from personal interviewing and mail questionnaire. If, however, the question reads, "What brands of soap do you use?" the personal interview is apt to bring more satisfactory responses. The personal interview will often bring back the complete facts, while the mail questionnaire usually obtains only the barest.

Towards the end of the questionnaire, you may wish to ask, "What make of car do you expect to buy when you turn in your present one?" By mail, the answers are likely to be, in large part, "Don't know." Yet an experienced investigator will get something like the following, "Like my car well, but the Y has a better appearance and a faster pick-up. Z has a fine engine, but I don't think it looks as well." The reasons given are entered as "additional information." This supplementary material may prove of greater value than the facts for which the survey was originally authorized. Extra information is difficult to obtain in the case of the mail questionnaire.

The personal interview secures more complete facts, it secures comments, it secures information about local situations. Taken as a whole, this extra information often forms the meat of the survey because it is the basis for determining trends. The mail questionnaire, except under unusual circumstances, collects only the more superficial facts and opinions. The usual purpose of a market survey, however, is both to collect facts and to determine trends—what changes in the product *will* cause future sales to increase, what advertising appeal *will* be best, what policy changes *will* increase dealer satisfaction.

Cost.—Complicated and long consumer questionnaires cannot be successfully handled through the mails under ordinary conditions. Excluding these, mail questionnaires have been known to draw as high as a 50-per-cent response or better; yet a 10-per-cent return is about the best which can be depended upon, even if the questionnaire, accompanying letter, and mailing list are carefully prepared. This means that each complete report costs forty cents for stamps alone. The inclosed return envelope may, instead of being stamped, be sent out under a mail permit, but this is apt to cut down responses considerably. Ten cents more per

State of	Governor
GOVERNORS' TELEPHONE SURVEY	
Question	*Reply*
1. The President's Committee desires to get in direct touch with the Governors to inquire if it can be of any assistance and to obtain information which can be passed along to other states.	
2. Mr. Governor, do you have a state committee? If so, who is its chairman and where may he be addressed? Several States, notably Ohio, have a committee representative of industry, labor, welfare agencies and government w o r k i n g through county committees.	
3. Is there any abnormal unemployment situation? What is the one outstanding feature of the situation in your state? Are the large cities of your state well organized?	
4. Will you not write me in some detail what you are doing so that I may pass it along to other states—particularly in reference to amount of unemployment, public works, and organization?	
5. Would you like to have a representative of the President's Committee call you so that we may be mutually helpful?	

Fig. 24

A telephone questionnaire used by President Hoover's Emergency Committee on Employment

returned questionnaire must be allowed for paper, envelopes, and (sometimes) a small reward for answering the questionnaire. One cannot figure the direct cost of obtaining a response by mail from this class of respondent at less than fifty cents per report.

When personal interviews are used, paper, envelopes, printing, stamps, etc., usually total less than five cents per completed report, and sometimes much less. The main costs are the investigator's salary and expenses. Traveling investigators must have their expenses paid, while resident investigators are reimbursed only for outlays which are ordinarily repaid to a man working in an office in his home city, such as local transportation, telephone calls, and the like. For simple, short consumer surveys, the interviewer will often average twenty-five satisfactory reports per day. (This is for house-to-house interviewing in urban sections.) Interviewers can frequently be hired at a figure which makes the total direct cost of interviews approximately the same as that for comparable results obtained through the mails. The type of ground covered makes a great difference in the cost. Responses from urban sections can usually be obtained more cheaply by interview, while from farm-homes the mail questionnaire is apt to be less expensive.

The office supervision for personal-interview and mail-questionnaire surveys is difficult to compare. As a matter of fact, the peculiarities of the survey affect the supervision expense more than the methods used in obtaining the facts.

Interviewing by Telephone.—The use of the telephone to make appointments for personal interviews or to check the validity of an interviewer's report is of long standing. Making entire interviews by telephone is, however, a more recent development.

Not enough is known about telephone interviewing to classify its advantages and disadvantages positively. The telephone allows for more discussion than the mail questionnaire. It is likely to cost less than the personal interview. The status of the person giving information is hard to determine, but, as in the case of apartment-house tenants, it is almost the only method of obtaining a direct contact. The use of the telephone in field research may be

Key Town Telephone Sales Areas

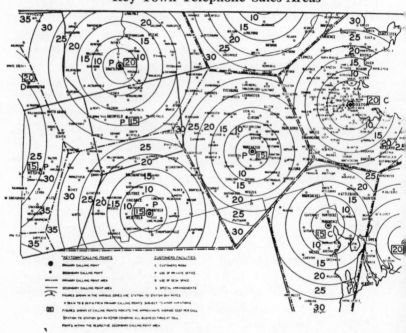

FIG. 25

expected to increase, but the limits of its effective use are not yet clearly defined. A questionnaire used in telephone interviewing is shown in Fig. 24 on page 84.

As an aid to telephone selling and interviewing, the American Telephone and Telegraph Company has broken down its lines into a "Key Town" system (see Fig. 25), so that primary and secondary calling points with the respective charges are shown for the entire country. A "sequence toll-call plan" has also been developed. Identification cards which give the privilege of charging calls anywhere may be obtained for investigators. In brief, the telephone companies are doing much to facilitate the use of telephones in interviewing.

Other Methods.—Other methods of obtaining information are discussed in Chapter XIII, "Field Tests."

PART THREE

MAKE–UP OF THE FIELD FORCE

Part Three explains the operation of field forces. It is a practical section dealing with the field workers and their management while they are employed during surveys. The selection of field workers is also dealt with.

The first chapter classifies field forces and compares the advantages of the various types in common use. Chapter VIII describes the qualities which are desired in field workers and the sources from which such persons are usually drawn. In Chapter IX the methods of operating traveling and resident field forces are explained, with emphasis upon the means used to obtain impartial results.

CHAPTER VII

TYPES OF FIELD FORCES

FIELD forces fall into two main classes—resident and traveling forces. Both should consist of skilled and experienced investigators. In addition, some firms use for gathering facts men who are primarily hired for some other purpose. The use of the sales force is one case of this. The conditions which pertain to the regular research force also apply to temporary investigators; so no attempt will be made to do more than indicate the appropriate use of the sales force in collecting facts.

The Resident Force.—A number of research organizations have investigators who live in different parts of the country and do field work in their respective territories. These people are prepared to do a reasonable amount of traveling, and they are, in many cases, capable of supervising assistants.

Specific training is given resident investigators for each survey through written instructions. At the beginning of his connection with the research organization, each one of these fact-gatherers, after proving his inherent ability, is personally trained by some member of the home-office staff until he can efficiently carry out the directions for a particular job. Fig. 26 on page 92 shows a typical resident force according to the geographic location of the investigators.

Resident investigators are sometimes required to travel far enough to cover their territory, which extends to the boundaries of the territories of the surrounding investigators, except in the case of sparsely populated regions. In addition, every resident force has at least two or three

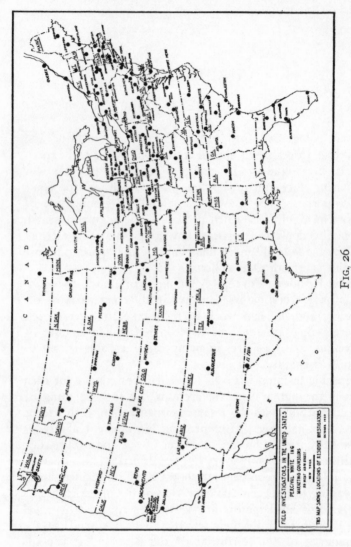

Fig. 26

A map showing the location of the resident investigators of one market-research organization

skilled investigators who are attached to the home office. These people can be used for extensive traveling; therefore the resident force has considerable mobility to cover the country and can, also, easily concentrate on one specific locality.

The Traveling Force.—The traveling force consists of a group of interviewers who are attached to the home office and reside in its vicinity. At the beginning of each survey they are given personal instructions and are often required to report at the office daily when the survey is local. These interviewers are sent to any part of the country which is included in the survey and often hire, train, and supervise assistants where intensive work must be done.

When marketing research was an unusual occurrence, this was the first form of organization. It offers a mobile force for gathering facts. There are many more traveling field forces in the country than there are resident ones, but the latter are very advantageous for certain purposes.

The Combination Force.—Some research organizations have both resident and traveling groups of interviewers, using either or both, according to the character of the information desired and the intensiveness of the survey. This makes possible any sort of interviewing which may be needed, but causes an unduly large overhead expense unless the volume of research is continuously great.

Resident vs. Traveling Forces.—In comparing resident and traveling forces, several factors must be considered, and the particular information desired often clearly shows which type of force should be used. In general, a resident force can get facts over a wide area more quickly than traveling investigators and at less cost. A resident force is very useful where widespread information is required at short notice. In one such case a report covering twenty selected cities scattered from coast to coast over the United States was delivered to a manufacturer by a market research organization with an able resident force seven days

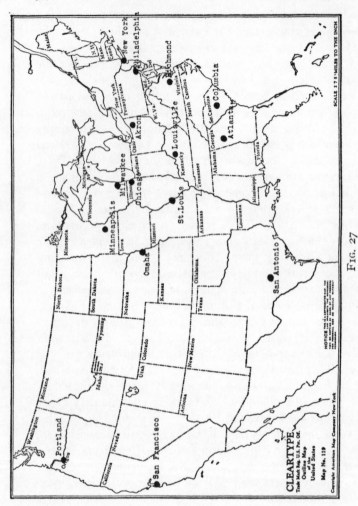

FIG. 27

A map showing the cities in which reactions were obtained in one week (from authorization of work to delivery of report) by the use of resident investigators, telegraph service, and air mail after the survey was ordered (see Fig. 27 on page 94, also Fig. 28 on page 96). No essential step was overlooked, but the work was speeded up. The result was indicative rather than conclusive, because the number of interviews which could be made was limited, even with liberal use of telegraph and air-mail service.

A traveling force has the advantage when the survey has to be highly coordinated or is very complicated. The more subtle the information needed, the more advantage there is in having a small group, or even only one interviewer, cover the whole territory. Comparisons between the attractiveness of two window displays exposed under conditions regulated by the investigators will be more dependable if the entire survey is handled by the same personnel. Likewise, high coordination is required to determine why there are fewer sales in one territory than in another where the conditions are apparently comparable. In addition, complicated surveys sometimes require so much preliminary training that only a few men can profitably be given the necessary preparation.

The second main element of comparison is the cost of the interviewer's transportation, telephone calls, postage, and the like. When the interviewer can go home every night, no living expenses are allowed. When he is on the road, however, all of his ordinary living expenses, such as hotel room and meals, must also be paid. The use of the traveling force thus entails a considerably greater cost for the same number of calls or for the same amount of field information. Unless there is some particular reason for employing the traveling force, the resident one is considerably more economical. The traveling investigator must usually be kept on a full-time basis, while very able resident investigators are often willing to do part-time work to add to their ordinary incomes.

The third contrast refers to the investigators themselves. The traveling force can be assembled before a survey is

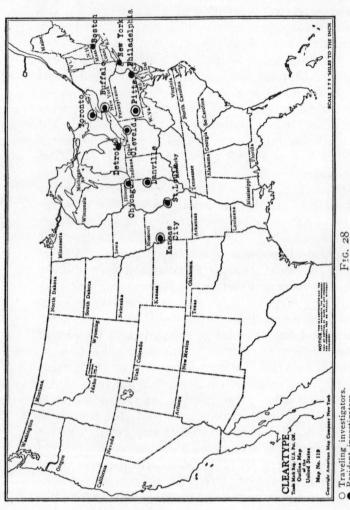

FIG. 28

○ Traveling investigators.
● Resident investigators.

This map shows the economical use of both resident and traveling investigators in the same survey. The resident workers did the consumer and dealer interviewing, while the traveling investigator interviewed the licensed local manufacturers after spending several hours with the resident investigators about the local situation

AUTOMOBILE SURVEY
General Instructions to Field Investigators

The purpose of this investigation is to collect information regarding the market for a new car called the ...., which will probably be placed on the market about the first of the year.

We are unable to furnish you with any picture of this car.

The first thing you will have to do after introducing yourself, etc., is to convey to the people you interview a mental picture of the car. This you will be able to do by memorizing the enclosed description of the car. If necessary let them read the description. You will note that this description is very brief, but it is hoped that the comparison on certain points with the .... and .... will enable them to visualize the .... to some extent.

In connection with this investigation there are five classes of people to be interviewed. They are:

	No. to be interviewed by you
1. Distributors of automobiles	8
2. Wholesalers	4
3. Manufacturers	0
4. Department stores	2
5. Specialty stores	25

It will be necessary for you to interview the total number of people listed against each class in the right-hand column above. Some extra questionnaires are also enclosed. These may be used if you can do so to advantage, but it is only essential that we receive the number specified. Special instructions are attached to each set of questionnaires.

Fig. 29
A page from the instructions sent to resident investigators during a recent survey

started and oral instructions given. Complete preparation for the problem to be solved can be furnished. The investigators may even go over sales records of the manufacturing plant. This may be very advantageous for certain types of investigation. The resident force, however, must receive instructions by mail and may not be so well prepared (see Fig. 29, on page 97, also Fig. 30 on page 99. For some surveys this is a disadvantage. On the other hand, oral instructions with discussions may give the investigator too much information and cause him to form preconceived opinions about the conditions which exist in the field. The nature of the problem determines which type of force is best.

The resident investigator gradually obtains rather complete information regarding his own territory. The traveling interviewer gets a better and broader view of the marketing field in general. Each of these types of experience has considerable value for particular kinds of surveys.

Use of the Sales Force.—The function of the salesman is to sell. In some cases, however, valuable information may be obtained from salesmen. The Jell-O Company, Inc., has used successfully a form called the "Traveller's Daily Report." The unusual items included in this form are best-selling jelly powder, next best seller, size of store, competitors' products in stock, window displays, cut-outs, danglers, and door signs. All of this information will come to the salesman's attention and be discussed with the dealer whenever a first-class selling job is done. This information is recorded at the completion of each call.

The Fuller Brush Company, which sells its products through house-to-house canvassing, has found that salesmen can do valuable work in learning the various uses to which its brushes are put. Likewise, important information has been obtained with respect to needs which the line did not fill (see Fig. 31 on page 100). Other firms have collected data in the same way.

PERCIVAL WHITE
MARKETING COUNSELOR
25 WEST 45ᵀᴴ STREET
NEW YORK
CABLES-DEODIKKA

November 26, 1929

Dear ------:

I am sending you herewith the necessary information, instructions and questionnaire forms for the interviewing work
about which I wrote you. These are:

        General Instructions
        Description of   (with suggestions as to use).
        sets of questionnaires with special
        instructions regarding each.

Your compensation will be at the rate of   per day,
plus any necessary expenses. It has been our experience on
this survey that the expenses should be practically negligible.

We desire that each question be fully answered. I realize
that it is not always possible to do this, but we have tested
these out pretty thoroughly and find that most people will take
the time to answer every question. Don't neglect any "comments"

We are very anxious, not only to complete this work at the
earliest possible moment, but also to have it up to our usual
high standards. We want you to do these interviews carefully
and accurately, but, of course, without spending any unnecessary
time on them. We have made a good many of these interviews and
know about how long they require.

We would like to have you write a general resume covering
the work when it is done. There is no form enclosed, but this
is not necessary, since it is to reflect your own reactions and
what the people you interview generally think, coupled with
your own thoughts on the subject.

        With best wishes, I am,

                        Yours faithfully,

FIG. 30

A letter accompanying material sent to resident field workers
when a survey is to be started

Thus while doing a first-class selling job, salesmen can collect information which may be of great value.

Limitations to the Use of Salesmen.—Salesmen have not been found satisfactory, however, for unearthing facts

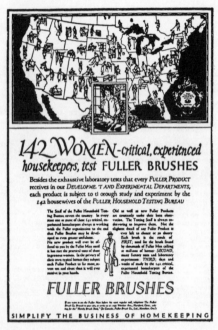

FIG. 31

The Fuller Brush Co. uses salesmen to collect information about the uses of its products and new items which might be added to its line. Every complaint received is passed back to the central office and the salesmen helped choose the 142 housewives mentioned in the advertisement reproduced above

which do not ordinarily come to their attention. The reasons for this are as follows:

1. The salesman's job is to sell. It is probably cheaper to let him do the job in which he is a specialist.

2. The basis of successful selling is optimism about the

product and the company which makes it. Successful research, on the other hand, demands the truth, whether favorable or not.

3. Salesmen often resent research as an extra and thankless job. This attitude injures the quality and the quantity of their work.

4. Salesmen, unless specially trained for such work, do not know how to conduct research interviews.

The Research Interview.—Successful research interviewing requires that the person giving information be at his ease. He should have no idea that he may be asked to buy anything. The standard introduction commonly is, "I am not trying to sell anything, but merely wish your experience with X." Where a salesman is unknown, selling habit tends to cause a positive type of approach and an attempt to influence the subject's views.

The person interviewed should be asked questions with no attempt to influence the answers through suggestion. Skillful interviewers, in fact, often manage to direct the conversation along the desired lines without ever letting the prospect know that he is being questioned. Successful fact-gathering depends upon eliminating the personal ideas of the interviewer. Successful selling, on the contrary, necessitates projecting the salesman's ideas to the prospects. The two methods are diametrically opposite.

When the information desired does not ordinarily come to the salesman in his regular calls, the best plan is to use skilled field investigators. Information from salesmen can be used to supplement such data, although every effort should be made to avoid antagonizing the sales force by requiring them to do too much such work outside their own line. Even where it is possible to use them satisfactorily, the question often occurs as to whether it would not be less costly in money and selling morale to have the salesmen do only selling.

Types of Information Adapted to Various Forces.— If a firm desired to know the effect of the introduction of a new model throughout the country quickly, the resident field force would be most desirable. If one of a group of competitors wished to learn what the others were planning to do as regards selling to a new voluntary chain organization, one traveling interviewer of great experience would probably be best. If window displays were to be tested by actually installing them in different localities, the traveling force would probably be able to arrange conditions in the most comparable manner. The sales force could learn whether the windows of the dealers could accommodate a slightly larger window display than the ones commonly used. Men trained in research interviewing, however, will usually be far better than those who may be on the company's payroll in other capacities, even though the latter are temporarily idle. Reports of interviews cannot be considered as establishing facts unless the reporters are themselves dependable as collectors of facts.

CHAPTER VIII

PERSONNEL OF THE FIELD FORCE

FIELD investigators collect raw material from the actual experiences of the persons whom they interview. What they report is the basis for drawing important conclusions. Therefore, every precaution must be taken to see that the facts gathered in the field are true and adequate. Field investigators must, therefore, be selected with the greatest care. Application blanks for field investigators used by market research organizations are reproduced in Figs. 32, 33 on pages 104, 105. The references are checked (Fig. 34 on page 108) and a personal interview with each investigator used is most desirable. Likewise, the potential investigator is usually given trial work before being used in a regular survey. Ideal investigators must have the following qualities:

Inherent Qualities.—

1. *Honesty.* Facts must be faithfully reported or the whole survey is worthless. Honesty is the most important requisite of field workers.

2. *Perseverance.* Interviewing is hard work. It requires confidence, resourcefulness, and continued effort to do a good job.

3. *Intelligence.* The field worker must be open-minded. He must look at each interview from a fresh viewpoint. He must have vision to picture the experience of the person interviewed. Intelligence is always required to size up people, to decide upon the method of approach, to perceive new angles of the situation, and the like.

4. *Judgment.* Is the experience described a "fairy tale"?

103

APPLICATION

Date ....

The information requested hereon will expedite the interview by precluding the necessity for asking and remembering this information; and if, at the end of the interview, it is mutually agreed that the applicant does not wish further consideration it will be destroyed. Otherwise, it will go into our private files for consideration of the applicant at some future time.

Name: Telephone:

Address:

Age:

Nationality: Religion:

Married or single: No. dependents:

Education:

Present (or last) position—firm name and connection:

What other positions held in past five years:

If employed, how soon can you go to work:

Will you travel:

References (give three, preferably previous employers or business associates):

Fig. 32

An application blank used by R. O. Eastman, Inc., when hiring investigators

Date....................................

```
┌──────────────────┐
│                  │    Name in full ...............................................
│                  │
│                  │    Street address ...............................................
│   PASTE PHOTO    │
│      HERE        │    City ................................... State ...................
│                  │
│                  │    Age ........................ Married? ...........................
│                  │
└──────────────────┘    Nationality ........................ Religion ...............
```

Are you now employed? ....

By whom? ....

Doing what kind of work? ....

....

Do you object to traveling? ....

What are your hobbies? ....

EDUCATION: What schooling have you had?...

....College degree? ....

Date you left college .... Correspondence courses ....

....Other education ....

Please indicate your experience and ability under each of the following subjects:

RESEARCH: Have you ever engaged in any commercial research? ....

If so, along what lines? ....

....

Describe any work you have done involving the use of statistics: ....

....

....

FIG. 33
An application blank for potential investigators. The references
are always checked

Have you copies of any commercial research reports prepared by you? ....

If so, please submit samples. We will return them.

ECONOMICS: To what degree have your education and past experience touched upon economics? ....

....

....

....

SELLING: Have you ever worked as a salesman? ....

In what lines? ....

With what class of trade are you best acquainted? ....

....

With what territories are you most familiar? ....

....

Have you ever done any sales promotion work? ....

Give details: ....

....

Have you ever done any contact work? ....

Give details: ....

....

ADVERTISING: Have you had any agency experience? ....

If so, outline that experience: ....

....

....

Have you ever worked in the advertising department of any national advertiser or publication?

....

If so, outline that experience: ....

....

WRITING: Have you had any newspaper experience? ....

If so, describe: ....

....

Have you ever written for publication? ....

Describe: ....

Have you had any experience in writing commercial or engineering reports? ....

Describe: ....

If so, please submit samples. We will return them.

MISCELLANEOUS: Have you a radio set in your home? ....

Would you be interested in getting other part-time work? ....

If so, what particular types would you be most interested in? ....

....

GENERAL COMMENTS: What, in general, are your opinions of field research, its applicability, and its future? What are your own qualifications and ambitions?

PERCIVAL WHITE   -   25 WEST 45TH STREET   -   NEW YORK CITY

Should the client's name be divulged? Can the interview be furthered by asking personal questions? Many problems such as these occur regularly in interviewing and can be successfully solved only through the use of sound judgment.

5. *Good Personality.* The interviewer must have an acceptable personality because he will fail unless he can inspire people with confidence. He needs to understand human

---

Your name has been given me as a reference by Mr. .... who is negotiating with me to act as my representative to do commercial investigation and research work.

I wonder if you would tell me how you would size up this man in regard to his integrity, accuracy, honesty, willingness to do hard tasks, and ability to create a friendly impression upon people he meets?

Any information you can give me will be greatly appreciated.

Yours faithfully,

PW:MKN

FIG. 34

Copy of a letter used to check the references offered by an applicant who wishes to do interviewing

nature and be tactful in order to obtain satisfactory information.

6. *Mobile Personality.* Each person interviewed, whether consumer, retailer, wholesaler, or expert, differs from all of the others, and the interviewer needs to fit his personality into the individual environment in which he finds himself. In order to avoid antagonism, he must make a distinct adaptation of his conduct to each person questioned.

7. *Courteousness.* The investigator should be courteous at all times, even when he is "thrown out." Successful interviewing is based upon courtesy, and a surprising amount of information is often gathered by the diplomatic interviewer.

8. *Good Memory.* The interviewer must be able to reproduce the tenor of a successful conversation. In the comments, particularly, it may be desirable to reproduce oral statements verbatim.

9. *Lack of Bias.* The investigator must be unprejudiced and take the facts as they are given without trying to influence the person interviewed. People of a domineering nature who color all conversation with their personal attitudes make poor interviewers.

10. *Powers of Observation.* The good investigator has an inquisitive nature and is constantly absorbing information. For example, he can add to the data received orally from a retailer, pertinent comments upon anything unusual in the store-window displays, counter arrangements, line of goods, etc.

11. *Physical Strength.* Interviewing is hard work and requires considerable endurance and physical ruggedness.

Acquired Qualities.—Some of the requisites given under "Inherent Qualities" are really acquired, but are of a nature which cannot be influenced very much in maturity. The following, on the other hand, can be influenced considerably at any time.

1. *Ability to Follow Instructions.* If one interviewer does not follow the prescribed method of recording data, his reports can be tabulated only with great difficulty. Field work requires that all instructions be followed to the minutest detail.

2. *Ability to Control Interviews.* If the person interviewed gets off the subject, the conversation must be turned back into the desired channel. When the requisite informa-

tion has been obtained, the interview must be concluded so that no waste of time takes place.

3. *Freedom to Travel.* Even resident interviewers may be required to travel. All field workers must make arrangements so they can travel at short notice.

4. *Accuracy and Neatness.* Reports must be accurate, precise, and neat.

5. *Dress.* A neat appearance is always desirable. An appropriate costume should always be worn. A suitable costume for interviewing business managers differs considerably from one for approaching foreign-born factory hands at their lunch hour.

Honesty of Field Workers.—The ideal field investigator does not exist. It is often difficult to find a sufficient number of even moderately good investigators. In any case, only persons of absolute integrity should be employed. Even under the best of conditions, it is impossible to supervise interviewing completely; so no person should be employed who does not enjoy the complete confidence of the executive responsible for the survey. Questionnaires may be filled out without actually making an interview. Replies to unanswered questions may be supplied from the investigator's fertile imagination. A consensus of opinion among the first few people interviewed may cause the investigator, instead of asking questions, to offer the already discovered opinion and suggest agreement. This is easier and quicker. Surveys can only cover a sample of the total market, and one dishonest investigator may make questionable the results of the whole survey. Checking is done, but the falsification might not be detected. Even if the dishonesty is discovered, there will either be a delay or a smaller number of questionnaires upon which to base conclusions. The basic requisite of the field worker is therefore honesty.

Idiosyncrasies of the Field Worker.—In fashion counts, where the subjects were selected at the discretion of the field worker, it was found that those were chosen whose appearance pleased the individual investigator. One worker would report only brunettes, another only blondes, a third all red-heads. The result was an unrepresentative sample, and the method had to be abandoned.

Prejudices, idiosyncrasies, and emotional characteristics of the field investigator are always a problem. One unfavorable experience of a man's wife five years previously may have the effect of making him prejudiced against, for example, all A. & P. stores, while he thinks favorably of all the other chain grocers. The ideal investigator has no such biases and is absolutely unprejudiced.

The honesty of a person may be unquestioned, yet, if a survey happens to run counter to a strong prejudice, the returns sent in by this person may be worthless.

Some "Don'ts" in Choosing Field Workers.—Research executives often have difficulty in securing a sufficient number of satisfactory field workers. In this contingency, persons who would not ordinarily be employed may have to be used. The following list of practical "don'ts" is of use in such a situation:[1]

1. Don't intrust the job to immature persons. They cannot recognize the importance of the work.

2. Don't select a person lacking in appearance. Your representative must convey the impression of the importance of the work.

3. Don't use your general office employees. These people are either too near the problem and subconsciously influenced by a desire to help you or they rebel against work of this kind.

4. Don't use your traveling salesmen. If they are worth their salt, they already have well-defined opinions about your business.

5. Don't use your officers (except research) to assist in field work. Their interviews are scattered and made without regard to your plans of tying one question to another.

[1] *Printers' Ink*, December 26, 1929, p. 49.

6. Don't use any person whom you would not personally trust.

Education of Field Workers.—Investigators with a college education are desirable. A good high-school training with an ability to speak and write the English language accurately is essential. The Department of Agriculture has found that college graduates who have majored in economics are unusually satisfactory.

Business Training of Field Workers.—Knowledge about marketing, advertising, retailing, and in fact about the whole field of distribution, is advisable. This need not be minute, but there should be a good foundation, which may have been obtained through study or experience. Without this foundation it is difficult to impart sufficient specific knowledge to the investigator before he goes out into the field. Thus business training in the newspaper, advertising, retailing, wholesaling, or related fields is always an asset. Its value depends upon the particular work which has been done, yet these types of activity yield a great many successful investigators.

Sources of Field Personnel.—Field workers come from numberless sources. The classification subsequently discussed is therefore of broad scope.

1. *Newspapers.* The newspaper is a source of two kinds of interviewers. First, in a large survey, a highly skilled investigator may borrow several men from a local newspaper's merchandise department, give them a short training, and have them do local interviewing under his close supervision. Second, men shift from newspaper work to field investigation. The newspaper gives them advantageous training in meeting strangers, in getting information in detail, and in remaining undiscouraged after a few turndowns. Its disadvantage is that newspaper work tends to encourage a freer use of the imagination than may be desirable in research interviewing.

2. *Advertising.* (a) Persons engaged in local advertising work acquire a great deal of local knowledge useful for field work, and often make excellent resident investigators. (b) National advertising work is a fine preparation because it gives a broad perspective of the distributive system and the way it works. Both types of advertising work help the investigator to see the problems to be solved from the viewpoint of the concern for whom the survey is conducted. Such conceptions of the problem and its conditions help materially in getting good results. On the other hand, advertising is a form of sales promotion and engenders a positiveness of attitude which is undesirable in field workers.

3. *Colleges and universities.* Professors of marketing have frequently been used as field investigators. This is especially true in the case of psychological tests, where the professor's classes are available to supply controlled subjects. Marketing classes under professorial supervision are sometimes employed to carry on local surveys. One important advertising agency tests students who desire to enter its employ. During the summer vacation between their junior and senior years, it uses them as field investigators. They are given an examination on each survey at its conclusion and these examinations have sometimes produced unexpected information of unusual significance to the client. Some agencies, however, feel that their problems are too confidential to risk the possibility of students discussing them and talking too much. Undergraduate students may be immature, consider the survey unimportant, or may lack discretion. They may be badly supervised, causing poor results. The exact opposite may be true, and there is no consensus of opinion among research executives, but all agree that undergraduate training in marketing is good preparation for field investigation.

4. *Other sources.* General business, selling, and many other forms of endeavor are good sources of field investi-

gators. The value of the training received from these sources depends upon the person and the particular work done. For example, selling is based upon convincing others rather than upon recording their opinions, yet salesmen know the distributive system well. One person may never get over his positive selling attitude; another can acquire an impartial attitude in a week.

5. *Unusual sources.* In rare cases, it is advisable to enlist the services of women's clubs, fraternal organizations, government employees, or the like. This is a case of using unskilled interviewers who are largely uncontrolled, yet certain facts can sometimes be obtained easily in no other manner.

Men *vs*. Women as Field Workers.—Field forces often have some women in them. Sometimes all the interviewing of consumers may be done by women. A comparison of men and women as interviewers is given below:

The advantages of using men as interviewers are:[1]
  1. Men are usually considered better for interviewing other men.
  2. There are few limitations as to the places where men can go or as to the time of their visits.
  3. Men are stronger physically.

The advantages of using women as interviewers are:
  1. For interviewing women in the home or about personal and domestic subjects, women get the best results.
  2. Women are treated more courteously than men.
  3. There is a lower turnover among women investigators.

Turnover in the Field Force.—Field investigation calls for initiative and perseverance. It gives the interviewer a valuable preparation for work in the field of distribution. Good interviewers are likely to aspire to an executive position in some related line of business. Adver-

[1] *Marketing Investigations*, by W. J. Reilly. Ronald Press, 1929.

tising, marketing, etc., furnish a great many field investigators who, after receiving valuable training in field research, return to more advanced positions in their original occupation. Turnover in the field force is rather high for that reason. Successful field workers are occasionally brought into the main office between surveys and trained in analysis and report writing. The main problem still is, however, to retain first-class interviewers after they have once been found and trained.

CHAPTER IX

ORGANIZATION OF THE FIELD FORCE

FIELD forces are organized in different ways, and each of these presents a different problem to the central office. The common kinds of organization are:

1. Resident force.
   (a) Resident investigators working in their home cities
   (b) Resident investigators traveling in the vicinity of their home cities.
   (c) Resident investigators using skilled and unskilled assistants.

2. Traveling force.
   (a) Investigators traveling from city of home office.
   (b) Supervisors traveling with a crew of investigators.
   (c) Investigators traveling and hiring local people to assist them as unskilled interviewers.

This classification is particularly important from the accounting angle. From the viewpoint of training and supervision, a threefold classification is sufficient—skilled resident, skilled traveling, and unskilled investigators.

Skilled Resident Investigators.—The resident investigator keeps in close touch with the central office, from which he is sent questionnaires and survey instructions. His work is in the field. He is given preparation for each specific survey by mail and reports to the home office by the same means. Unquestioned integrity and training in market research are essential. In fact, resident investigators are often people who have had previous experience as traveling investigators before becoming permanently located.

Basic Training.—When a satisfactory investigator has been found, he is sent a manual of field research which has been carefully prepared at the central office. In this, each step in market research is analyzed, the importance of field work is emphatically shown, and the duties of the interviewer are outlined in detail. A potential resident investigator living within reasonable distance of the central office is then brought in and shown all the processes through which a survey passes. He is instructed in the art of interviewing, accompanies an expert investigator during a few interviews, makes some interviews himself under the observation of his tutor, has these criticised, and this procedure is continued until his work is reasonably efficient. During his first few surveys, only simple work is required, and sample reports must be sent in to the home office for correction and return before the interviews are allowed to count toward his quota. Resident investigators, when first employed, may not be skilled interviewers, but they invariably should be persons of maturity with considerable experience in some related field.

When the new investigator lives at a great distance from the home office, the training is given through correspondence-course methods at the expense of more time and effort. A page from the general instructions of one research agency is given in Fig. 35 on page 118, Form No. 1.

Specific Instructions for Field Work.—Resident investigators receive questionnaires accompanied by detailed specific instructions as to how the interviewing is to be conducted. A complete statement of the information necessary for doing efficient work is included in the mailed package as a separate document. The investigator must study this carefully before going out to interview. Questionnaires with interviewing instructions are given in Figs.

36, 37 on pages 119, 120. A letter which accompanied a questionnaire and broadly outlined the work is given in Fig. 38 on page 121.

Interviews: All interviews should be made IN PERSON, unless you are instructed to use the telephone. You can of course sometimes use the telephone to help locate the right person to see. Much time can often be saved in this way, particularly in locating specific types of dealers.

Accuracy: This means not only a correct transcription of what the person interviewed has said, but an accurate statement of the facts as they exist. If the person interviewed is lying, or uninterested and careless in answering, makes contradictory statements, etc., it is your duty to attempt to get at the real truth of the situation, or discard the interview and replace it with another. Follow the SENSE of the interview sufficiently to catch a contradiction or inaccuracy of statement, and try to get it straightened out. Be equally sure that you record correctly the FACTS which have been given you. Infinite harm can be done to us and our clients through misstatements either careless or wilful. Our clients will come back at us for explanation of any statement which appears contradictory or questionable.

Complete Information: While this cannot always be obtained an explanation of its lack can always be made. Do not send us questionnaires with BLANK questions. Every question should have either an answer, a line drawn through it to show that it does not apply in that particular case, or a reason given for the lack of answer. Do not attempt to FORCE an answer, as such information is most likely to be incorrect. On the other hand, the amount of information you get from any interview will depend entirely upon yourself. You can draw out the respondent by your method of carrying on the conversation.

Repetition of Information: Do not feel because a statement, either in an answer or a comment, has been recorded on a few questionnaires, that there is no use going on repeating the same thing. You are recording the exact substance of EACH INTERVIEW and it is the number of repetitions that will be weighed in analyzing the investigation.

Additional Information: Do not consider yourself confined to the questionnaire or outline. Some of the greatest value of the survey often comes to light in your comments.

FIG. 35

Page from general interviewing instructions for resident investigators. These are used by the Arnold Research Service and apply to all surveys

Traveling Investigators.—The traveling investigator receives his final instructions for the survey as well as his general knowledge of market research in the central of-

A

1. Name of Concern: John Doe & Company, (American Furniture Store Synd.)
   Address: 100 Main Street,
   City: Jackson, State: Mich.

2. Person interviewed (write name):

   Proprietor _____ Buyer E. A. Brown

   Manager _____ Clerk _____

   Adv. Mgr. _____ Other _____

3. Give names of:

   Buyer E. A. Brown

   Mdse. Mgr. J. C. Smith (all Hqtr. N.Y.)

   Adv. Mgr. L. S. Jones

4. Kind of store: (check)

   High grade dept. store ( ) Installment House ( )
   Popular priced dept. store (✓) Dry Goods Store ( )
   High grade furn. store ( ) Excl. Floor Covering ( )
   Popular priced furn. store ( ) Other (state) _____

5. a. Relative appearance (interior): Good ( ) Fair (✓) Poor ( )

   b. Relative size of store: Large ( ) Medium (✓) Small ( )
   (Meaning for that town or similar surrounding towns.)

6. Class of trade catered to:

   Above average (✓) American (✓)
   Average (✓) Negro ( )
   Below average ( ) Native white (✓)
   Laboring class ( ) Foreign ( )

7. Degree of store's importance to local floor covering business
   (that is, its relative importance in that town.)

   Major ( ) Moderate (✓) Minor ( )

8. Is the store known for price cutting among its competitors? Yes ( ) No (✓)
   (If so, check this with a neutral source: Give Name: _____

9. What types of floor covering do you stock?

   Oriental (imported) rugs ( ) Velvet rugs (✓)
   Sheen type rugs (✓) Tapestry rugs ( )
   Wilton rugs (✓) Narrow carpet (✓)
   Axminster rugs (✓) Broad carpet (✓)

10. Approximately what percentage of your rug business is done in rugs retailing at;
    (based on 9' x 12' sizes)

    Under $40 50 % Between $40 and $70 30 % Over $70 20 %

FIG. 36

A questionnaire for which special interviewing instructions appear in Fig. 37

If you find that a store is not a retail store, but *only* a wholesaler or jobber, do not go any further with the interview, but merely write across the face of the entire blank "Wholesaler." If they do some retail selling, write under "Other (state)" of Question 4 "Also Wholesaler," and continue with your investigation.

"Dept. store" means department store.

"Furn. store" means furniture store. A furniture store is one which carries *any* home furnishings, but is distinguished from a department store in that it does not carry other items.

"Dry Goods Store" means one which specializes in dry goods, piece goods, blankets, bedding, and so on, but is not a department store.

"High Grade Store" means one which has excellent standing and sells to the better trade.

"Popular Priced" means a store feature price rather than quality.

Question 5, dealing with the appearance and size of the store, is to be checked in accordance with your opinion and observation. Please note that by relative appearance, we refer to whether the interior is well arranged and neat, and as to whether, in your opinion this dealer, compared with other dealers, displays his goods to advantage. As to the size of the store, you are to gauge this also in relation to other stores in that town, or similar surrounding towns.

Question 6. Check here what class of trade is catered to, opposite the proper definition. You can get this information from a floor walker, if in a department store, or possibly, an intelligent looking clerk. If you do not feel satisfied with the answers you can check up on them when interviewing the buyer, proprietor, etc., or else when you interview a competitor.

We want you to use an unusual amount of care in making sure that all of the information throughout this questionnaire is as accurate as possible. In this question, you should also find out and indicate on the card, whether the bulk of their business comes from Americans (white or negro), or from foreigners.

Question 7. Again you are here to decide as to the store's importance among its competitors. We want to know the standing of this dealer among his competitors so that our client can pick out the one that he wants to carry his merchandise. This explanation is true, as a matter of fact, for the entire questionnaire, as that is the main reason why this study is being made.

Question 8. This question is addressed to you, the interviewer. You are to decide after having made inquiries, whether or not this store is known for price cutting. *Do not ask this question of the dealer interviewed.* You may ask competitors for their opinion. By price cutting, we mean the practice of under selling legitimate competition. We do not mean seasonal sales such as are put on from time to time by good stores, but a store which has the reputation among the trade for cutting prices and profits unduly, just to get the business. If you have gathered such an opinion, be sure to check this with a neutral source, such as the Advertising Manager of a local newspaper.

FIG. 37

Special instructions for conducting a specific survey. The questionnaire to which these instructions apply is given in Fig. 36

PERCIVAL WHITE
INCORPORATED
MARKETING COUNSELORS
25 WEST 45ᵀᴴ STREET
NEW YORK
CABLES-DEODIKKA

December 12, 1929

Dear Mr. Smith:

We are enclosing the following material relating to a survey of anti-freeze liquids:

          1. Instruction Sheet
        100   Consumer Questionnaires
         20   Dealer Questionnaires
          3   Envelopes

We want you to do three full days' work on this job. (This time need not be spent consecutively.) This work must be completed, and all questionnaires and your summary mailed not later than the evening of December 18. If you can finish sooner, it will help us materially.

If you are going to be able to do this job, according to all our requirements, please write immediately to that effect. If you are not going to be able to do this job, please telegraph collect to that effect immediately.

Remuneration will be at the rate of $___.__ per day. This includes all expenses, except postage. Send us a bill for your time when you send your summary, and add charges for postage. We will send a check promptly.

We have had quite a call for automobile interviews, lately, and expect more presently.

Yours faithfully,

FIG. 38

Letter outlining work to be done in a survey. This accompanied the special instructions and questionnaires to a resident investigator.

fice. A manual is presented to the prospective investigator; he is shown surveys as they pass through every process; he is trained in interviewing by an experienced man and usually does interviewing of a simple nature under supervision at the start of his active field work.

In the case of large and important surveys, the investigators may spend a day in the factory to see a product made. As a rule, a few interviews are made locally in order to eliminate any difficulties in the questionnaire, the technique of writing up the answers, or any similar problems.

As a final step, routings are examined, quotas are set, the arrangements are made for receiving mail and additional questionnaires while on the road. After the traveling investigator has left the home office, keeping in active contact with him is a major consideration.

Supervision of Investigators.—Skilled investigators are not usually personally supervised in the field. Their work is checked and edited by the central office. In the case of an intensive study in one locality, an exception may occur, yet, if such an interviewer requires close supervision, he is not worth the money he costs.

While skilled interviewers get more and better comments than those who are unskilled, sometimes, where only simple facts are required, unskilled interviewers are used. They may be employed and supervised by either resident or traveling investigators. A variation from this occurs when a supervisor from the main office takes a crew around with him. In this case, the men may be skilled, semiskilled, or unskilled field workers.

Where only a brief training is given, the emphasis is laid upon the specific survey to be conducted. A lack of general training in market research and interviewing is compensated for by strict supervision. The supervisor conducts a few sample interviews with each man and spends his time correcting reports, checking the men at work, and closely watching the whole procedure. Entire responsibility for the survey rests upon the supervisor. He keeps the records of the group and reports to the central office.

Nothing must be left to chance in using unskilled men. They have no experience to help them. The object of the investigation must be made clear; the best time to make calls must be given; the importance of obtaining comments must be emphasized; the impartial point of view must be continually called to attention; routes must be minutely worked out; a system of reporting to the supervisor must be established; minute instructions for filling out questionnaires must be prepared; identification for the workers must be provided; the selection of subjects must be made; above all, the importance of the work must be emphasized at every opportunity.

Compensation.—Field workers are usually paid by the week, day, or hour. Payment by the completed questionnaire or other unit of accomplishment often affects the results unfavorably. The quality of the work done is the most important thing in investigations, and piece-rate payments emphasize quantity. Also, the unknown factor in field work is the human element, the individuality of the subjects approached. Ten good interviews are sometimes made during a period of good fortune in the time it might take to make five poor ones. Quotas are set upon the basis of experience, but the quota in field work is usually a variable one, because the quality of the information gained is more important than the quantity, except under very unusual circumstances.

Reports from the Field.—Questionnaires are mailed daily to the central office. In doing local work, the investigator also reports in person or by telephone. The returned questionnaires are accompanied by a statement of progress and of any unusually interesting facts. When the work in a locality is completed, a summary of the results is included.

ARNOLD RESEARCH SERVICE

New York—Chicago

LOCAL TIME RECORD

(Do not enter traveling time, out-of-town working time or traveling expense on this sheet.)

Supervisor_____ No. Job_____ Date Rec'd_____ Date Comp._____

City_____ Quota_____ No. Calls Made_____ No. Comp._____ No. Incomp._____

Interviewer	Mon	Tue	Wed	Thur	Fri	Sat	Total		Rate	Total Salary	Expense			Total Amount Paid Worker
							Days	Hrs.			Fares	Postage	Telegr.	
Totals														

Amount of Advance _____

Balance Due _____

(Do not record lunch hour on here. Record number of working hours only for each day.)

FIG. 39

A local time and expense sheet. Out-of-town traveling expenses are entered on another sheet. Fig. 40

Questionnaires which are filled in during the day are checked before mailing. A supervisor is required to check all of the reports turned in by his crew.

Accounting Practice.—The central office follows ordinary business practice with respect to expense accounts. When an investigator is working locally, he receives no allowance for ordinary expenditures—carfare from home to business district and return, lunch, etc. If any unusual expenses are incurred, however, as for additional transportation to facilitate interviewing, these are paid back to him. Fig. 39, on page 124 is used for entering local time and expenses.

When an investigator travels, all of his ordinary living expenses are paid, as well as actual transportation costs. Advances are frequently made to defray these expenses. Many field research agencies bill all traveling expenses direct to the client, for whom the survey is conducted, the survey charge being based upon service exclusive of traveling expenses. This practice forces the central office to have the investigators who travel make out their expense accounts in such a way that ordinary expenditures (*i.e.* telephone calls, stamps, etc.) and traveling expenses can be segregated. Fig. 40, on page 126, shows a Traveling Time and Expense Sheet while Fig. 41, on page 127, illustrates a sheet used for charging traveling expenses to clients.

The central office quotes a flat price for the survey. Its problem is to keep within the estimated costs. Master sheets for a complete survey are shown in Fig. 42, on page 128. The records are kept in such a manner that it can easily be determined whether or not the work is coming in on time. This is important because field research is usually sold not only upon the basis of a fixed price, but also a fixed time limit. The great problem is to get the work done promptly without lowering the efficiency of the field work or the value of the analysis of the field data which have been gathered.

ARNOLD RESEARCH SERVICE
New York—Chicago
TRAVELING TIME AND EXPENSE SHEET
(Do not record local time expense on this sheet.
Make separate sheet for each town visited.)

Supervisor_____   Job. No._____   Quota_____   Date Rec'd_____   Date Comp._____
From_____   To_____   Left-day_____ Arr.-day_____   Ret. Start-day_____ Arr.-day_____   ___hr. ___hr.   No. Calls Comp.____   No. Calls Incomp.____

Inter-viewer	Mon	Tue	Wed	Thur	Fri	Sat	Total Days hrs.	Rate	Total Salary	Train Fare	Auto Mileage	Hotel	Meals	Local Fares	Tel & Postage	Inc	Total Amount
											$	Days $	$				
Totals																	

Amount Advance _____
Balance Due _____

FIG. 40

Traveling expense and time sheet. Local time and expenses are entered on a different sheet. Fig. 39.

ARNOLD RESEARCH SERVICE
New York - Chicago

Job No._____

D I R E C T C H A R G E M A S T E R S H E E T

Survey:_____   Client:_____

Date_____

CITY	Travel			Hotel			Meals		Misc.	Expense
	Mi.	Rate	Am't	Day	Rate	Am't	No.	Am't		

TOTALS

TOTALS

FIG. 41
Sheet used to charge traveling expenses direct to client when
arrangements have been made to do this

JOB ESTIMATE SHEET—PERCIVAL WHITE INC.

Client:　　　　　　　　Estimate by:　　　　Date:

	Hr.	Cos.	Personnel for each task												Total hours	Total cost	Actual hours	Actual cost
			H	C	H	C	H	C	H	C	H	C	H	C				
Plan entire work																		
Contact client																		
Prepare questionn.																		
Supervise field work																		
Check edit questionn.																		
Mailing to field																		
Interviews summar-izing																		
Tabulation																		
Hand																		
Coding																		
Punching																		
Tables																		
Recaps																		
Chart work																		
Typing																		
Supervision																		
Report																		
Assemble and draft																		
Editing																		
Binding number-ing																		
Other																		
Total est.																		
Actual																		

List here cities in which interviews are to be made, with number in each, or other pertinent information:

FIG. 42

Master sheet showing allocation of expenses for a complete survey

Obtaining Uniform Results.—Securing uniformity of results, so that the data obtained by different investigators may be compared, is the ideal in actually conducting the field work. Identical questionnaires and interviewing instructions are used. Reports are edited as they come in from the field. The classes of persons to be interviewed are specifically defined, sometimes particular firms or persons being listed. Suggestions for improving the work are constantly being made. In fact, a large number of minute records are made so that the material from one interview may be compared with that from every other one. A considerable number of these regulations will be discussed in Part Four, "Work of the Field Force."

PART FOUR

WORK OF THE FIELD FORCE

Part Four deals with the actual work done by the field investigators. It includes rules and procedure for the worker from the time he receives his instructions until he has mailed his survey summary. Special emphasis is laid upon techniques which have proved successful.

The first chapter in this section describes how to prepare for the interview, locate desirable respondents, and decide upon an efficient method of procedure. The two succeeding chapters explain how to make interviews and record the facts which are obtained. Desirable technique is minutely analyzed. The final chapter deals with the problem of conducting field tests and other types of group interviews.

CHAPTER X

THE PRE-INTERVIEW WORK

BEFORE the field investigator begins his interviewing, there is a considerable amount of work which has to be done in the locality to be covered. Regardless of the training received before going into the field, the material in this chapter applies almost equally to both resident and traveling investigators.

Survey Instructions.—If the survey instructions can be interpreted in two ways, telegraph the home office for explanation. The same rule applies when the practical application of definitions is not clear, or when classifications do not cover all cases. The small additional cost of a telegram or two is unimportant when compared with the possibility of having a number of useless or faulty reports.

Traveling investigators are trained for each specific survey by the home office. Resident investigators usually receive their instructions by mail. In both cases, however, the worker should obtain additional information for himself if he believes his preparation insufficient. The home office will be glad to cooperate in this. In many cases, the training may seem adequate in advance, but actual field work may prove it insufficient. The worker should immediately take steps to obtain the needed information before doing further interviewing, as it will otherwise be impossible to report facts and opinions satisfactorily.

Local Situation Survey.—When the interviewer knows his instructions and is in the locality where his immediate work lies, the first step is to analyze his local environment. The public library, the Chamber of Commerce, or the merchandising department of the local newspaper can be consulted. One or all of these will be able to furnish pertinent local information. The residential sections of the

FIG. 43A

A section of a map which divides up the local market in such a way as to help an interviewer plan his work.

city according to income groups can be found; the names and addresses of dealers, wholesalers, and manufacturers can be ascertained. Inclusive maps which analyze the local markets are sometimes available, as is illustrated by Figs. 43A-B, on pages 134 and 135.

Routes which involve a minimum of wasted time and

effort can be worked out by the interviewer. Likewise, the
distribution of interviews can be arranged in advance, according to the instructions for the survey. If the work is
intensive, the route will follow areas of greatest density
for the group to be considered. Probably a representative
picture only is required. Then the routing should be planned
to cover the whole area. One hundred Class C consumer

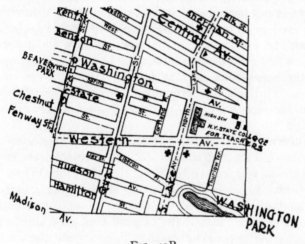

FIG. 43B
"SECTION E-7"
One division is assigned to an interviewer as his exclusive working
territory

interviews should be divided among the several sections
where Class C consumers live and not be confined to one
of them. When no specific instructions are given, the interviews should always be spread in this manner. Individual
calls may well be restricted to one in a block or related to
the population of the block, permitting a certain percentage.
If the "best" stores alone are to be covered, care should
be taken to follow this plan. If "typical" stores are to be
visited, some of the poorest stores, as well as the best, must

be included. When the field worker has mapped out his problem carefully, economical routing is not difficult to plan.

Classification of Respondents.—The survey instructions will indicate into what classifications respondents are to be divided. In practice, there may be difficulty in applying these directions. The border-line cases are important. When a decision has been reached as to the classification of cases not specifically covered in the survey instructions, the method of arbitrary decision used should be written down and memorized. In addition, the data about border-line or new classification cases should be immediately mailed to the home office so that any necessary changes can be made. Through this procedure, consistency of classification for each interview and among interviewers is maintained.

Information about Prospective Respondents.— Knowledge about desirable prospective respondents is just as necessary as knowledge about their location. Where any particular business executives or specified dealers are to be interviewed, personal information is sometimes obtainable. This is not usually the case but even general information may be of great importance. For example, the workers in a certain factory town live in two distinct districts. One of these is so close to the mills that the men return for the midday meal while the other is too far away for this. When the men return at noon, the large meal of the day is eaten then; therefore the women of this district usually have spare time in the afternoon while those of the other district have leisure in the morning. For house-to-house interviewing among consumers, such information is vital. The investigator should learn all he can about the prospective respondents and their habits. In practice, something significant can usually be learned by advance inquiries and the first few interviews should yield many valuable data about the local people.

Identification.—Each field worker must be given means of identification. A card of the research agency may be sufficient. Sometimes it is not. The investigator must be supplied with complete means of identification. He must also be prepared to use these in such a way as to inspire confidence in a prospective respondent. This requires previous thought. The identification data must be ready, as well as information about the research agency, the purpose of the survey, etc. A hesitant respondent is almost invariably lost if the interviewer is not able to supply identification easily.

Hours to Call.—The best time to approach a prospective respondent is when he or she has leisure. In general, the best hours to call are between nine and eleven in the morning and one and five in the afternoon. Ordinarily, the time before nine in the morning and after five in the afternoon is relatively unproductive. If there is work other than actual interviewing to be done by the investigator, it will pay to make his calls during the most productive hours. The type of respondents desired and their habits will, of course, determine when leisure periods occur. For some purposes, the evening hours are best. During a hot spell in the summer, one interviewer found that the most productive time for approaching housewives was from seven until nine-thirty in the evening, when they were sitting on their porches to enjoy the evening coolness. Another made an enviable record by interviewing lower executives at public golf courses early Sunday mornings while these men were idly waiting for their turn to tee off. A study of the local situation will often show some method of utilizing all of the day in productive interviewing.

Memorizing Questionnaires.—The investigator should know his questionnaire, regardless of whether or not he is permitted to have it in sight while questioning respondents. This usually involves memorizing the questions. An exception occurs in the case of long technical questionnaires, where, even if the whole were memorized, the quantitative answers would have to be entered as given. Here the worker must know and understand the questionnaire thoroughly.

Questionnaires aimed at either the investigators or the respondents should be memorized unless their length makes it too difficult. Respondents, once started on a subject, may answer three or four questions without further impetus. For example, the question, "What soap do you use?" may bring a response: "X soap because it washes well in this hard water and is cheap. I tried Y soap for a while, but it won't work well in this hard water." The investigator must be able to ask an appropriate second question which will not force the respondent to repeat previous answers. In brief, regardless of the complex or multiple responses brought forth by the early questions, the investigator must know what questions on his list yet remain unanswered, without interrupting the conversation to examine his questionnaire minutely.

Quotas.—The central office ordinarily sets a daily quota of reports for the interviewer. Sales quotas, all too often, are impossible goals to strive for, but the research quota is meant to be reached. Therefore, it should be reasonable and based upon the past daily returns of each interviewer in similar surveys. Two things, however, should be remembered. First, quality is always to be preferred to quantity in research. Quotas, on this account, usually have a minimum number of interviews which is expected and a larger figure which presumably ought to be reached. The minimum figure is necessary to make the sample sufficiently large, and is insisted upon even if more time must be spent than was originally intended. Second, the number of satisfactory reports per day varies considerably even after allowing for obvious factors like weather and holidays. Ten first-class reports may be obtained in one day in the time it takes to obtain three mediocre ones on some other day.

The interviewer should not become discouraged unless he is failing to meet his quota when he experiences no difficulty in making contacts. Even in such cases, the quality of the reports may compensate for the small number. Every effort should be made, however, to meet the quota minimum. In fact, the investigator should plan and route his work to meet the quota and to check up on his progress in

---

NUMBER OF REPORTS

We have set 20 *first-class* interviews per day as a minimum quota. Throughout the trial work in the New York area our investigators have done much better than this. As a result we are inclosing a number of extra questionnaires, because we think that you will exceed your minimum quota by a comfortable margin.

(In the particular survey from which the above instructions are quoted, the investigators made, on the average, 24.6 satisfactory consumer interviews per day.)

FIG. 44

A minimum-maximum quota where the lower number of reports is required and the higher number hoped for

so doing. A minimum-maximum quota is shown in Fig. 44.

Use of Telephones, Automobiles, etc.—Making appointments by telephone, conducting interviews by telephone, traveling by automobile, and other similar methods of speeding up the field work are used by investigators when the saving of time effected appears to warrant the expenditure. Unless an investigator abuses such privileges, the home office commonly allows him to use his own discretion in the matter. Costs of field work are calculated upon the lowest possible basis; therefore a telephone call should not be made or an automobile used instead of the street car unless some decided advantage results. If a considerable saving in time is accomplished, even long-distance telephone calls may be justified. The burden of proof, however, always rests upon the field worker when he makes such unusual expenditure.

Allowances for the use of automobiles, as for all other expenditures, are made on a cost basis. If the worker uses his own car, he is paid on a mileage basis. Out-of-pocket expenditures are reimbursed in all other cases.

In planning the local work, quick transportation and communication to increase the efficiency of the investigation should always be considered. The home office is concerned primarily with the cost necessary to obtain adequate facts and not so much with the minute methods of this expenditure. Decision must always depend, however, upon whether methods of increasing speed will secure enough and better facts in the allotted time to pay for the expense.

Rules of Conduct for Interviewers.—The investigator should be guided by the following general rules in conducting his survey :[1]

1. Do not argue.
2. Do not contradict.
3. Do not insist.
4. Do not be familiar.
5. Do not act as a detective.

These rules are summarized in the positive statement, always be courteous. Courtesy is essential for successful interviews. In research, it is especially important because the field worker is asking a favor of every person whom he interviews.

---

[1] *Standards of Research*, by J. F. Carroll. Meredith Publishing Company.

CHAPTER XI

INTERVIEWING

THE purpose of interviewing is to gather information. Every person approached is an authority who is being consulted and who is expected to give valuable facts or opinions to the interviewer. Let the authority do the talking. Questions need be asked only when the conversation wanders or a new phase of the subject requires introduction. The interviewer should cultivate the attitude of an interested listener who desires to be deferential. When the respondent is a high ranking executive, it is easy to assume that an oracle is speaking, yet successful interviewing requires this same attitude when the respondent is of the humblest order.

The field worker may be better educated than the persons whom he consults; he may be paid more than they; he may hold a social position higher than they. Nevertheless, the respondents, in the aggregate, presumably know more about the particular questions which they are asked than do the interviewers and the home office executives, or no field survey would be necessary. Thus the receptive attitude must be maintained during all interviews.

Approach.—In making contacts the interviewer must immediately inspire confidence and give an impression of sincerity. Frankness is the best policy. Each individual worker will soon learn the best way to approach people. In general, a statement of purpose, identification, and the reason for answering should be at once presented.

The statement, "I am not selling anything," is one effective way to begin an interview. The subject must be given that information in one way or another. Following this, the positive purpose of the call must be clearly explained. In this statement of purpose, both positive and negative, the worker should normally identify himself with the research organization by which he is employed. A business card may be proffered or merely the name of the organization mentioned.

After the general purpose of the call has been stated and the identification of the interviewer established, the next step is to induce the subject to answer the desired questions. The problem to be solved is stated and the subject is asked to help, it being shown that his personal experience or opinion is considered valuable. Assistance by the prospective respondent may be frankly asked as a favor. Current news of interest about the line of business in which the subject is employed may be told. The general facts found up to that time by the interviewer may be given. There are numerous plans used to get people to talk.

Respondents should always be made to feel that they have received something from the call as well as given information. Even when the approach is based upon asking a pure favor from the "authority," benefit to the respondent can be shown. During interviews with dealers and other business men, comparisons between the respondent's business and competing ones in other towns can be mentioned. care must be taken not to repeat private information from one man to another, and the interviewer must always be prepared to handle the bugaboo of private information being carried to a competitor. Innovations in window display, new articles seen in other stores, suggestions as to this and that, etc., can, however, be given. Even in the case of housewives, an interest can be created for the interview.

Length of the Interview.—In order to avoid wasting time, respondents are sometimes given successive questions one after the other as they occur on the questionnaire.

When the conversation lags, it is often a better idea to direct the conversation back into the desired channels in a more diplomatic way, such as: "Your experience with X interests me, and I would like a little more information about it. How was turnover with X?" A respondent, if merely guided loosely, is likely to cover all of the questions as quickly as could be done by insisting on the printed order. In addition, the information is likely to be more spontaneous and of better quality.

The time element in research is an unavoidable evil. The research spirit is slow but sure. So much of the interviewer's time is spent in making satisfactory contacts that he cannot afford to cut an interview off short until that particular source of information has been exhausted. No interview which is still yielding applicable facts should be summarily ended even though information sufficient to fill in the questionnaire has been obtained. On the other hand, no time can be wasted. Time is secondary until all of the pertinent data have been secured. Then the interviewer should make as quick an exit as is diplomatically possible.

Client Company's Name.—The interviewer will sometimes face the question, "But for whom is the work being done?" The prospective respondent may insist, for example, upon knowing the name of the company producing the article which is being investigated. The reporter may in some cases answer that he is willing to give such information, but prefers to wait until the completion of the interview, so that the respondent will not be prejudiced in his answers. If such a reply is made, the reporter must be sure to live up to his word.

The producing company's name can usually be safely given out at the end of an interview. Sometimes this is of distinct advertising value. On the other hand, if the producing company wishes its name concealed, there is little need to worry. The cases where inquiry is made as to the firm hiring the research agency are rare. In many of these

cases, the name of another intermediary company is satisfactorily received. This occurs often when an advertising
agency is instructed by one of its clients to hire a market
research agency to conduct a field survey. Investigators can
truthfully say, in many cases, that they do not know for
whose benefit the survey is being conducted, but understand
that it is being made for an advertising agency, a bank,
etc. It is considered good practice for the central office not
to make known to field workers the name of its client.
Little trouble is usually encountered in such cases.

Should the Questionnaire be in Evidence?—There is
considerable difference of opinion as to whether or not the
questionnaire should be shown during the interview. R. O.
Eastman, of R. O. Eastman, Inc., market analysts, states
the position of those who favor showing the questionnaire,
in the following words:

Our theory and our practice are that we want to dignify
the study from the beginning and get a serious, interested
attention. When the impression is made on persons giving information that these facts are wanted for a very serious purpose, the answers we get are dependable.

People, on the other hand, unquestionably talk more
freely when there is no indication that their responses are
being written down. An obvious written record makes
people reticent and thoughtfully careful. Some surveys call
for spontaneous reactions without reserve. Others require
deliberation on the part of respondents. The method of
approach will be planned accordingly.

Long technical questionnaires must be shown, because
the quantitative and technical answers have to be filled in as
received. Some research executives, however, prefer to have
their investigators show questionnaires as little as possible.
A practical general rule is to attempt to interview without
showing the questionnaire, but to bring it out if necessary.
A facetious respondent may be toned down; questions

which need only a check mark for answers may be filled in, and other advantages may be obtained through bringing out the questionnaire. The questionnaire, however, should never be displayed to such an extent as to interfere unduly with spontaneity and freedom of conversation on the part of respondents.

Technique of Non-questionnaire Interviewing.— Since respondents often give answers to several questions in one paragraph and in mixed-up order, it is very difficult to keep mental track of the exact progress of the interviewer. Notes on the questionnaire or a brief of it must be accessible. When informality has been adopted to give freedom to the discussion, it is essential that the briefed questions be inconspicuous, so they may be outlined on the back of a used envelope or the inside cover of a magazine.

Some successful interviews occur without the knowledge of respondents that they are being made. In a motor-car survey, people were often interviewed at filling stations when they did not really know that they were being questioned for any definite purpose. Such unsuspecting responses are often extremely valuable to business executives. In retail surveys, investigators can sometimes accomplish the same result by making small purchases and starting a conversation. Two or three such apparently casual discussions are always good checks upon facts which are being obtained through other methods of investigation.

Indirect Method.—Many questionnaires will include one or two questions for which it is very difficult to obtain satisfactory answers. When this occurs, an indirect method of approach is desirable. For example, the question, "What make of X machine do you expect to buy when your present one is worn out?" may receive several types of unacceptable answers. At the end of the interview the subject might be asked what he thinks about the new machines put out by A, B, and C. It is likely that this will yield information concerning the make of future replacements and, what is more important, the reasons for this choice.

Poor answers can often be handled best by passing right on to the next question for the time being. Near the end of the interview, the poorly answered question can be taken up again. One successful device is to appear to close the interview and to ask the troublesome question in a casual manner as a seeming afterthought.

Figures of a nature which may be considered confidential are often obtained indirectly. For instance, figures on total volume of business may be calculated from the volume of sales of one line and its percentage of the total. A grocery wholesaler may be asked the volume of soap sales per month and what share of total sales this represents. From a number of such data a reasonably satisfactory calculation can be made. If the investigator makes a rough mental calculation, he can casually say to the wholesaler, "Then your total volume must be about $100,000 (or the like)?" and it is quite probable that the exact figure will then be given.

"Doubtful" Respondents.—Interviewers will run across rare cases where respondents are obviously giving false information. More frequently the investigator will feel, but without tangible evidence, that the information is exaggerated or distorted. In both cases, the reports should always be so marked. A facetious attitude on the part of subjects may occur; enthusiasm may cause men to exaggerate; a deliberate attempt to deceive may even occur. In bad or obvious cases, the interview should be quickly terminated, and the partial report destroyed. In questionable cases, the report should be completed and marked "doubtful," with explanatory notes if needed.

Every research organization tries to weed out false data through editing, yet it is forced to trust its field force greatly in this respect. Field workers hate to throw out complete interviews, but this must be done when the facts are questionable. The sacrifice is not much, since turn-downs in interviewing seldom average more than one per day and contacts are not unduly hard for the competent worker to make.

Interviewing "Named" Subjects.—The names of persons (or firms) from whom information is to be requested are occasionally furnished to the field investigator. Some of these specified persons may refuse to give the requested data. If such a situation arises, the interviewer should keep right on with his list, so that his schedule for the bulk of the work is maintained. One or two individuals must not be allowed to stop the course of the survey.

Research organizations, except under the most unusual conditions, do not expect the field worker to make a successful contact with every person on a specified list. In fact, forced or unwilling answers to questions are usually not wanted. If in doubt about the home-office policy, the investigator should continue his scheduled work while communicating his troubles to the survey executive. Ordinarily, data about the firm or business in question is acceptable when obtained from other than the person specified. Often, entirely different persons or firms can be substituted, so that data from all of the "named" group need not be secured. The important thing is to get the bulk of the work done before bothering unduly with troublesome cases.

Interviewing Consumers.—Consumers, especially housewives, are quick to give excuses. It is the interviewer's duty to present his case quickly and interestingly within a very few moments. If possible, he should endeavor to gain entrance to the house (or office). In any case, it pays to make the approach carefully and not be in too much of a hurry to ask the first question.

An interesting constructive presentation must be made—ask a favor, pay a compliment, explain the problem, etc. The housewife's confidence must be obtained within a minute or two if the interview is to be satisfactory.

The advantage of entering the house in consumer work is that time ceases then to mean so much to the prospective respondent, and the easiest way to remove the investigator is to answer his questions. Sometimes it is possible to examine the articles which are the subject of the survey in the consumer's home. For example, a glimpse may be obtained of the cupboard when the housewife checks up on the size of X purchased or the number of brands of Y she uses. Classifying those interviewed is also easier if you can see their homes. It is, therefore, quite an advantage to be allowed to enter the consumer's house. A good approach is necessary to secure this opportunity.

Due to the use of strong methods of salesmanship and "follow-ups," consumers often close up like clams when written records of what they say are made. Before the questionnaire or notebook appears, three things should have been explained to the consumer: 1. The questionnaire or notebook is merely a convenient means of recording the information given. 2. The facts obtained will not be used in a personal manner. 3. There will be no "follow-ups" or endeavor to sell. As regards names and addresses, consumers are unusually squeamish; therefore these should be requested last with the "no-follow-up" idea emphasized.

Interviewing the Trade.—In interviewing retailers, wholesalers, and the like, the investigator commonly passes through the active business part of the concern. In a moment or two the able interviewer can pick out some point upon which to compliment the dealer or to make a suggestion. For example, the caller may say, "That counter arrangement displaying X is a good one. How did you work it out?" or, "Have you seen the unusual way that Z of Smithtown has arranged his store?" A little current trade news has probably been learned by the field worker and he can relate this to the dealer. The good investigator, in fact, always has something of value to offer. This should be given to the dealer early. After this, an ordinary approach will usually result in a hearing.

When in a store, the investigator can often answer some of the necessary questions himself. For example, the brands of baked beans carried by a grocery store can be learned by looking. Examination is also likely to disclose which brand of beans is featured. Sometimes entirely unexpected data of importance are thus obtained. The dealer is in many ways easier to approach than the consumer because his business is fundamentally based upon human contacts.

When the brands carried is one of the questions, it is advisable to have a list of the common brands made out on scratch paper. The ones carried can then be checked off without undue expenditure of time or interruption, and the importance of each brand can be indicated by numbers— 1, 2, 3, etc. Unusual brands can be marked for attention by a statement such as, "I haven't that brand on my list. Is it a local one?"

Telephone appointments are not usually necessary in interviewing consumers and dealers. If one particular contact is not made, another can be easily substituted. In the case, however, of large dealers and wholesalers, the number of satisfactory prospective respondents is usually limited. Arranging for an appointment is therefore advisable. Some research agencies write to a few especially desirable people and prepare them for a definite appointment which will be asked for by telephone. More commonly, the interviewer is allowed to arrange his own contacts by telephone. Where certain known persons of limited number are desirable subjects, the telephone is very useful in obtaining hearings and in saving time which may be wasted if the respondent is busy.

Interviewing Business Men, Professional Men, and Experts.—Business men, professional men, and experts commonly make their appointments by telephone. The reason for an appointment is best explained in advance.

Sometimes this cannot be done, but it is a good rule to follow, especially if the number of desirable subjects is at all limited. In important cases, appointments are sometimes made by telegraph or long-distance telephone. The more important the executive, the more important it is to have an appointment. There are cases, of course, when it is wise to call without announcing one's intention of doing so.

There are two rules about business interviewing. The first is to do everything possible to discover the correct man in the organization. The home office, ordinarily, supplies this information in the case of very important executives. When the desired man's name is unknown, a telephone appointment is difficult to arrange. One plan is to ask the firm's telephone operator or reception clerk about the correct person to approach, and have her request an appointment at a certain hour. By using any interim for making other appointments, a minimum of time is wasted. The second rule is, if the correct person cannot be determined, approach the highest ranking man who might be the desired person. The man at the top can at least definitely tell the interviewer whom he should approach.

Higher officials are difficult to make appointments with, yet they are at the same time most intelligent and are usually willing to talk if properly approached. For one thing, they have salesmen or similar representatives on the road for whom they desire courteous treatment. For another thing, many of them have learned that interviews frequently help them, either through information which the investigator gives them or through the different angle of approach to their own problems which the interview suggests.

Various techniques are used in approaching business men. A crude but successful scheme is the following: "I have a problem. Will you help me? It is [explanation]. I feel that you are in a position to help solve that problem and shall appreciate your cooperation. The X aspect of the situation occurs in your field," etc. State that you have a problem, ask for assistance, begin with a compliment about the man's ability to help you, and keep talking about the problem until the man's interest is aroused. Nine times out of ten, this procedure will secure a hearing.

Other methods sometimes obtain equal or better success and the experienced investigator is able to adapt his approach quickly to the peculiarities of the individual whose assistance he desires.

CHAPTER XII

RECORDING FIELD OBSERVATIONS

THE field investigator must report the facts as they actually exist. He must be able to reproduce the sense of every interview. He must quote respondents word for word in the case of significant remarks. Every bit of information which is obtained must be reported because it cannot be used until it has been transmitted from the investigator to the home office. The interview, in fact, is worthless unless the data obtained are effectively recorded. Three major rules are to be followed in reporting field work: 1. Make whatever notes are necessary during interviews, so that actual figures, etc., will be accurate. 2. Write up complete notes (if these are to be transcribed in full later) or complete each questionnaire immediately after the close of each interview, and never make a second interview without having recorded the facts from the first. 3. Report all applicable material obtained, even if it seems relatively unimportant.

Taking Notes During Interviews.—Even if the questionnaire is in evidence, the investigator will have to take some notes. Answers requiring merely a check or the name of a brand may be filled in at the time, but longer answers cannot be written down in full during the interview without seriously interfering with the discussion. It takes an interviewer's attention to keep up the respondent's interest, and a complete cessation of the conversation from time to time invariably leads to a discussion with loose ends or to the consumption of an undue amount of time. Some reporters have the gift or knack of remembering even a rather long conversation and being able to record it accurately after the interview is over. Such people, of course, have a great advantage.

The "Old-envelope" Method.—An admirable statement of the "old-envelope" method of note-taking has been published under the name of Æsop Glim in *Printers' Ink* :[1]

Assume that you are to interview an executive. Have a clear picture of what the interview is to cover. Take a used envelope or some papers which have been in your pocket for a time and copy your questionnaire in pencil. Follow those instructions exactly. A leading word or two will be enough to identify each question. Instead of writing, "What make of automobile is owned," put down, "Car owned." You talk with the executive and cover everything you can think of in the course of your conversation. The interview is almost at an end. Then say: "Mr. President, I made some notes of the different things I wanted to take up with you. I think we have covered them all, but let me look to be sure." Now take out the used envelope with your penciled notes and start to read aloud each question. "The make of car you own— you told that, it is XYZ. The number of miles you get to a gallon—you told me about ten miles. Here is something we did not take up—the tires which came as original equipment." You get an answer to that question and then proceed to check back on every question. Do you recognize what you have done? First of all you permitted your prospect to tell you his story in his own way. A paper and pencil did not scare him. He talked freely because his remarks were not being made a part of the record. When he finished, he unknowingly went through your questionnaire and you in turn confirmed your recollection by having him check his answers.

Follow that method and you get the right kind of interview. It is not deceitful and tricky. You merely remove an imaginary impediment which could prevent the one interviewed from giving the information as he desires to give it.

In the case of a long questionnaire or a series of figures, it is impractical to conceal the questionnaire and pencil.

[1] *Printers' Ink*, December 26, 1929, p. 44.

When it becomes necessary, these are brought out and used in a natural manner and again placed in a pocket as soon as possible. The principle is to have the formal questionnaire and the recording of written answers play as small a part as possible during the conversation with the respondent.

The "Magazine" Method.—Both permitting the questionnaire to be in sight at the beginning of the interview and strenuously endeavoring to conceal all evidences that a record of the interview is being made are extremes of technique. The "magazine" method lies between and has the advantage of flexibility.

The interviewer provides himself with the current number of a common magazine. On a convenient part of it he briefs the questionnaire in pencil. The outside of the cover is often used. A few questionnaires are placed in the middle of the magazine, and the interviewer starts out with the magazine rolled loosely under his arm or in one hand. When a prospect is approached, the magazine draws no unfavorable notice because the prospect himself often carries magazines. A stub pencil which can be concealed in one's hand is carried by the interviewer. In talking, many people are accustomed to change around things which they carry. As a result, the investigator can refer to his briefed questionnaire with a minimum of disturbance. Notes can be similarly written down. No direct attempt at concealing either the reference to the questionnaire or the note taking need or should be made. The respondent himself has probably written many notes on magazines which he was carrying. The magazine may, when necessary, be opened to the printed questionnaires, usually without interfering with the respondent's attitude. The "magazine" method allows the adopting of whatever methods of procedure seem most desirable for the particular respondent during the interview itself. The formal questionnaire may be produced, no notes may be taken, or various in-between expedients may be resorted to. The magazine itself offers a means for carrying questionnaires without folding them, provides something to write upon when filling in the questionnaire after the interview has been terminated, and furnishes adequate scratch paper.

In interviewing executives, the "old-envelope" technique is considered better by many people because the interview takes place within an office and both parties are sitting. The magazine may appear unnatural and undignified. In other cases the "magazine" method has marked advantages, because there is almost invariably the need for making a few notes. In all methods the interviewer has the opportunity to check up on inconsistencies before closing the discussion, and he ought to do this in every case.

Entries on the Questionnaire.—Immediately after an interview and before another is made, regardless of the temptation to do otherwise, the interview just ended must be written up. Experience has shown that honest and complete records will not be made otherwise. The rule is to write up the record of the interview as soon as the respondent is out of sight. The facts as they are obtained are difficult enough to handle without having errors due to inaccurate memory.

Questionnaires are of two types, considered from the recording angle. First, those upon which actual questions with blanks for the answers appear; second, those which give only a topical outline to be followed by the investigator. In the first case, the blanks for answers should all be filled in immediately, so that the particular record is completely finished before another prospect is approached. In the second case, the brief notes taken during the interview should be expanded and organized according to the topical outline, so that the writer's memory will not be strained when the report is finally typewritten (see Fig. 45 on page

156). These notes need not be grammatical, but they should answer all salient points.

STEEL WOOL PRODUCTS INVESTIGATION
OPINIONS OF DEPT. STORE BUYERS

Summary of the interview: "I do not think that this product will sell to our class of trade. I tried it out in two departments, the kitchen furnishings and the general household departments, and it did not move."

Sales appeal: "The copper product seemed to attract the women's attention. I believe it was 'the color appeal' and the fact that it was different from the steel color. In every case, those interested did not buy when they ascertained the price, and this was largely due, I believe, to the fact that they are familiar with the large package of the X-product and steel wool obtainable at ten cents."

Disadvantages of product: "Some women seemed afraid to buy this product, as they had had painful experiences with cut fingers from using steel wool. Several also mentioned the fact that the steel wool and the X-product broke up into small particles and stopped up the drain pipes of their sinks to such an extent that they had to have a plumber come in every few months and clean out the trap."

Comments: "The only way I see that this product would sell is to make it more individualistic, as to package or shape. The material is good, as I thoroughly tested it out, but I believe that the copper product in the form of a ball or sponge would be the one to concentrate on."

FIG. 45
Portion of an investigator's report with a topical outline questionnaire

Leave No Blanks.—All questions must have an answer. This may merely be a line through a question which does not apply; it may be a statement, "Unable to answer," or a brief explanation of why the subject was unwilling to answer. Every blank space is on the questionnaire for a purpose and it must be filled in truthfully.

The home office wants the facts; therefore it would rather receive a questionnaire with the notation, "Unwilling to answer," than a forced statement from a respondent which, more likely than not, is incorrect. A person who is compelled to make statements against his will commonly does not give the truth or, certainly, the whole truth.

Repetition of information is irksome to the investigator. Data, however, should always be repeated for every case where found. The repetition may be of even greater importance than the fact itself. It is the repetitions which are measured when the tabulating is done.

Editing Before Mailing.—Reports often appear complete when they are written up in the field, when, in reality, they are not. Interviewers should always go over their reports before mailing them to the central office. Before being sent, each report should be legible, consistent, intelligible, accurate, and complete. Figures, especially, should be clearly written. The people who tabulate are not supposed to be experts in reading hasty scrawls. No questionnaire can be used without troublesome delay when there is doubt about the writing and figures.

Additional Information.—The interviewer should seldom, if ever, allow himself to be limited by the questions appearing on the questionnaire. These are considered important, it is true, but they are aimed at a specific problem. No product or producer, however, faces such limited trouble. Additional information may apply to other problems or indirectly to the one being probed. The purpose of the survey is to get a complete picture of the situation in the localities studied. In certain surveys, the "extra" material has been of more importance than that elicited by the specified questions. In other cases, the lack of comments and additional data has led to false conclusions. These facts do little good, however, unless they are reported in every case where they occur. The first-class interviewer gets all of the facts pertaining to the local situation and records them.

Specified questions, regardless of how carefully they are worked out, commonly result in a limited number of facts and a little about opinions or trends. The unstandardized material, which may be vitally important in the case of trends and changes, must be obtained by the field worker through his own initiative. Many times, such information is forthcoming when the specified questions are asked. It should invariably be recorded and, possibly, investigated by asking other respondents an extra question when the opportunity occurs. If so many additional data are collected that the blank is insufficient, use the back of the questionnaire, and indicate on its face that you have done this.

A number of years ago, a certain company was planning to build a tire factory. A questionnaire was used to determine the relative popularity of fabric and cord tires. Tabulation of the returns showed that fabric tires were used by a great majority of people. A fabric-tire factory was built and subsequently operated at a great loss. When the survey was made, people were using fabric tires but planning to replace them with cord tires. If the survey had been made by skilled interviewers, even though an applicable question did not appear on the questionnaire, this fact might have been revealed.

Summaries.—The summary is essential in field work. It should give the investigator's reactions to the entire situation and be written at the close of active work in one locality. If more than one locality is covered, there should be a summary for each and a final summary of the entire situation as the worker sees it. Summaries have several purposes. First, they are checked with the tabulation.

Second, they can explain unusual facts about the tabulation. Third, they provide a place for all information not otherwise taken care of. Fourth, they are of primary importance in picturing the local situation as a unit and in showing sectional trends.

MINNEAPOLIS, MINNESOTA

1. Architects as a whole deprecate the advances made by asphalt shingles and would cooperate with wood shingle promotion, but buyers of asphalt shingles are not the people who go to architects.

2. Lumbermen and building material dealers, although enjoying volume of business, on composition shingles predict a swing to wood shingles within a few years.

3. Intelligent buyers are skeptical about the "fire-tests" on asphalt shingles and I am informed sub-rosa by a Minneapolis architect that the local test was a fiasco.

4. Although one of the largest manufacturers of composition shingles is located here in Minneapolis the architects, builders and contractors criticize the quality of the composition shingles and were it not for their excellent exploitation they would be at a disadvantage. Nothing but consumer demand keeps up their sales.

5. Not enough attention has been paid to
   Home Modernizing Bureaus
   Small Home Building Bureaus
   Individuals who write for home magazines
   Press propaganda by lumber people.

Fig. 46

A portion of an investigator's summary made at the end of a survey

The summary should be concise and clear. There should be a place for everything of note which has appeared during the survey. Even though material is on the questionnaire, its essence should be included here. The goal of a first-class summary is such completeness that it could, for all practical purposes, be substituted for the questionnaires and their tabulation. The summary is where the interviewer's work will show quality and analytical ability. The central office must determine the value of an interviewer largely by his summaries and the remarks appearing on the individual questionnaires (see Fig. 46 on page 159).

The summary should specifically include the following facts:

1. Geographical distribution of interviews.
2. Racial and class group distribution of interviews.
3. Peculiar local factors which explain facts collected.
4. All outstanding points of the local situation.
5. Brief of all the facts and opinions obtained.
6. Trends which seem to exist.
7. Ideas of the investigator, stated as such and separated from the factual material.

Use of Summaries.—The tabulation, remarks on questionnaires, and the summary should show correlation. The tabulation may show that brand X was carried by the most dealers. The summary may show that the domination of brand X was greater two years ago and is rapidly decreasing. Comments and remarks from the individual interviews ought to show the same trend, and give reasons. The tabulated facts must check with these or be interpreted to show the trend. In some cases, a lack of unity between tabulation, comments, and summary clearly shows the need for further work.

Consumers in one residential section may use Y product much more freely than any other group interviewed. The investigator may learn that this is due to the neighborhood dealer pushing this particular brand. This fact should be given in the summary. Consumer facts may depend upon dealer attitude; company policy may determine dealer attitude; certain salesmen may have undesirable peculiarities; advertising may have reached one consumer group more

USE OF REPORTERS' DAILY SUMMARY SLIP
(Form No. 76)

Fill in name of survey and number in spaces provided.

Number of days worked should be the actual number of days up to the evening when reports are being mailed in.

Number of reports should be separated by classes such as dealers, consumers, jobbers, etc. Any additional classifications of questionnaires can be written in similar spaces at the top of the two remaining columns.

Multiply the quota on any given questionnaire (see specific instructions on each survey) by the number of days worked and set down in the spaces opposite the word "quota."

Under "Previous Total" bring forward the total number of interviews mailed into the office to date, but not including the reports sent on the day this summary slip is made out.

"Reports Herewith" is to be the actual number of reports of each kind mailed in with this slip.

"Total to Date" is total of "Previous Total" and "Reports Herewith."

Fill in name of town from which reports are being mailed, the date, and the reporter's name.

Attach this slip to all interviews being mailed at the time, or include it in the envelope in such a manner that it will not become lost.

Reporter's Daily Summary

Attach to front of reports and mail in daily. Keep carbon or carry total onto next sheet.

Survey.. No.....................

Days work to date ....

Reports:	Dealer	Consumer		
Quota				
Previous total				
Reports herewith:				
Total to date				

Mailed from ....

Date...................... Reporter...

Form 76

FIG. 47

Reporter's daily summary form and instructions about its use, as employed by R. O. Eastman, Inc.

than the others. Any number of peculiar conditions may exist which affect the facts gathered. All of these conditions should be fully stated in the summary.

Interesting phases of competition, price-cutting practices, in fact, all things affecting the product and its manufacturer locally, are significant. These facts may appear inapplicable or unimportant to the investigator, yet some of them may be vital. All should be included. The summary is often the best means by which the survey executive can picture the local situation as a unit. It is the flesh with which the tabulation skeleton is clothed. Summaries are often quoted in final reports and the investigator should realize that they are vital factors in reaching correct conclusions. Incidentally, a field worker is most often judged by his summaries.

Mailing Reports.—Completed interviews should be mailed daily. Each package should include a statement of the number of interviews sent and their classification (see Fig. 47 on page 161). The summary should accompany the last shipment of interviews unless this would cause the delay of a business day in receiving the package. Interviews are sent in by first-class mail.

The reports completed during the first day of the survey should be sent to the home office immediately, so that all troubles and mistaken interpretations can be corrected as soon as possible. Also the home office may find that additional questions are necessary. Reports should always be sent in promptly, but this is of greatest importance at the beginning of the field work when adjustments may be necessary to obtain uniformity throughout the field force.

It is preferable to typewrite summaries and reports which are based on topical outlines instead of on set questionnaires. In this case, two carbon copies should be made. The original and the first carbon are mailed to the home office in separate packages to insure their arrival. The second carbon is kept by the investigator until he receives

word that no further information is necessary. It sometimes happens that the summary of one worker may
indicate unexpected facts about which the other workers
will be questioned, necessitating an amplification of the
summary.

CHAPTER XIII

FIELD TESTS

FIELD investigators have been required to do little field testing in the past. The value of proved products, policies, appeals, and the like is, however, gradually becoming widely recognized; hence considerable work of this nature will unquestionably take place in the future. This chapter will attempt merely to indicate the commoner types of field tests and to illustrate them briefly.

Individual Tests.—The individual test is really one type of interview. The investigator makes a contact in the usual way and then proceeds to display the product, container, etc., and ask the respondent for his opinion. A regular questionnaire may or may not be followed. The prospect's reactions are carefully recorded and reported, as in the case of an interview. The Parker Pen Company used an interesting procedure in testing its belief that an oversized colored fountain pen would be acceptably received by the public. Each investigator was equipped with a dozen fountain pens, varying in size and style, and all black except two new models. These pens were displayed on a tray and the investigator was instructed to ask prospects: "Will you pardon me, please, if I ask a question? I am not selling pens, I am merely finding out what kind people like. It will help me a great deal to have your opinion. Won't you try these pens and see which suits you best?" No further questions were asked, but the investigator was instructed to answer all questions asked him about the pens. The prospect's reaction to each pen tried and the effect of its price, if asked, were recorded as soon as the interview was over.

A manufacturer of grocery products was uncertain about the best shape and color for the container of a new product. Various containers were prepared and investigators displayed these in grocery stores scattered over the country. Customers of these stores were asked which container pleased them best, and were given an inexpensive package of another product as a reward at the end of the individual test. The results were twofold, the choice of the best container among those considered and an interest in the new product on the part of the consumers.

One plan is to leave a sample of the product with the consumer for trial. This procedure was used for a small cleansing device when the people approached had never used it. As the cost of the device was small, the sample was promised to housewives as a reward for reporting their experiences in using it. The results from the data thus collected indicated the advertising appeal most suitable for obtaining new consumers and clearly showed the need for an additional type of outlet.

In the case of a small portable electric lamp, the article was too expensive to be left as a gift, but consumers who tried it and reported their experiences were allowed to buy the lamp (a new product) at a reduced price. This survey yielded valuable data regarding changes which would improve the product, and indicated the prices which consumers would be willing to pay for such a portable lamp.

At least two calls are necessary to complete a report in this type of work, hence the prospect must agree to later calls during the first one. Respondents are therefore harder to locate, yet, once successfully approached, they take a greater interest in the investigation than is usually the case in ordinary interviewing.

Group Tests.—Group tests differ considerably from interviewing. In some cases, no personal contact is made with the respondents; in other cases, individual contacts are made in advance of the test, which is then conducted for all members of the group at the same time.

Late in 1929, the Coca-Cola Company conducted a test to determine the relative attention value of ten window displays.[1] Four of the displays were miniatures and six were regular cut-outs. Six windows were selected for the test with the six regular cut-outs, and four windows for the four miniatures. Ten locations in Atlanta were selected with care. Seven were downtown and three were residential. Of the seven downtown locations, three were at congested corners where circulation was the heaviest in the city. Two hours was considered an adequate test for a regular display at any one location, while three hours were allotted to the miniatures. The day was divided into fixed periods. At the end of each period every display was changed to a new location until each display had been tested in every one of the windows assigned to its size of display. Thus no display received any advantage by reason of the location at which it was tested.

The tests were conducted by twenty selected college men, each equipped with a circulation clock. One man clocked the number of people who passed during each test period. The other clocked the number of people who turned their heads to look at the display and also the number of those who not only looked, but stopped to examine it. The man clocking the lookers and stoppers placed himself in a position behind the display, so that he could carefully note those who actually turned to look at the window. That each display might receive a fair count, every pair of clockers was scheduled so that they clocked a new location and a new display each period. Thus every display and every location was clocked by every pair of clockers.

The results of these tests for attention value are given in the following table:

[1] *Printers' Ink*, January, 1930, p. 145.

Name of display	Number passing	Number looking	Per cent looking	Number stopping	Per cent of lookers stopping
Regulars:					
A..........	6,490	1,222	18.8	18	1.5
B..........	6,498	1,272	19.6	18	1.4
C..........	6,410	740	11.5	41	5.5
D..........	6,791	806	11.9	18	2.2
E..........	6,778	1,248	18.4	29	2.3
F..........	7,570	871	11.5	28	3.2
Total..........	40,537	6,159	15.2	152	2.5
Miniatures:					
W..........	6,435	1,660	25.8	92	5.5
X..........	8,477	1,374	16.2	61	4.4
Y..........	7,994	1,560	19.5	66	4.2
Z..........	5,934	1,169	19.7	123	10.5
Total..........	28,840	5,763	20.0	190	3.3
Grand total....	69,337	11,922	17.2	342	2.9

The miniatures displays made a better showing than the regular sized ones. Two of the miniatures (W and Z) proved to be the best of the ten displays from the attention angle. Other factors besides attention value are, of course, to be considered in selecting a window display, but it cannot carry its selling message unless people will look at it.

A fashion count has recently come into vogue. At intervals of a week, for example, a statistical count of the color of dresses worn by women may be made. Some select restaurant may be chosen, and the number of women entering the establishment between noon and two o'clock recorded. One worker may keep track of the total number of women, another of the number of women wearing a dress of a certain color, a third of the number wearing certain types of hats, etc. From such data gathered over a period of time, trends in fashion can be determined and reasonably accurate forcasts can sometimes be made.

Group tests may sometimes be used to get a large number of responses quickly. For example, the investigator may arrange to present his questionnaire to a group of college students and have the students write out answers individually. With "Yes" and "No" questions, an adequate sample for a rather large university might be collected in an hour or two. Under favorable circumstances, a Chamber of Commerce lunch or some other gathering might be used for the same purpose.

Psychological Technique.—Marketing research is sometimes faced with the necessity of learning facts the validity of which depends upon continued similarity of conditions during the test. The technique of controlling conditions when human subjects are being studied is being developed rapidly by psychologists. Psychological technique applies to both individual and group tests. A plan for measuring the confusion between similar trademarks offers a simple but indicative illustration. This method was devised by R. H. Paynter and is standard for its purpose:[1]

A set of 20 trade names typed on slips of paper was shown to a subject at the rate of one slip per second. Immediately afterward he was given a pack of 40 slips made up of 20 trade names that had not been in the first set, 10 that had been in the first set, and 10 that were imitations of the remaining 10 in the first set. He was instructed to pick out those that he had seen before. Every time that an imitation was picked out as having been seen before, one score of confusion was checked against that imitation. After all the trade names had been thus tested, each imitation could be given a confusion value in terms of the number of the persons (or the percentage of all the persons tested) who were confused. If enough cases of varying degree of confusion were at hand,

---

[1] *Psychology in Advertising*, by A. T. Poffenberger, p. 311.

it would be possible to select a series of them that would range all the way from zero confusion to 100 per cent or complete confusion in steps or intervals of 5 per cent or 10 per cent. The scale shown in Table 3 was prepared in this way insofar as the data permitted. The first column of figures in the table gives the order of the trade marks arranged according to the percentage of persons confusing the imitation with the trade-mark, and the second column of figures gives the actual percentage of confusions. The smallest degree of confusion is indicated by 1 and the highest degree by 15. It will be noted that the actual amount of confusion ranges only from 5 per cent to 85 per cent instead of 0 per cent to 100 per cent.

TABLE 3, SCALE OF CONFUSION VALUE OF TRADE NAMES

Original	Imitation	Order	Percentage confusion
Welcome...........	Welcome A. Smith...	1	5
Golden Charm.......	Charm.............	2	10
Yusea..............	U-C-A.............	3	20
Royal Irish Linen.....	Royal Vellum.......	4	30
Beats-All...........	Knoxall...........	5	35
Shipmate...........	Messmate..........	6	40
Six Little...........	Six Big...........	7	45
Carbolineum........	Creo-Carbolin.......	8	50
Momaja............	Mojava...........	9	55
Grenadine..........	Grenade...........	10	60
Muresco............	Murafresco........	11	65
Cottolene..........	Cottoleo...........	12	70
Dyspepticure........	Dyspepticide........	13	75
Siphon.............	Siphon System......	14	80
Nubia.............	Nubias............	15	85

Table made by R. H. Paynter.

An analysis of decisions shows that a confusion of at least 30 per cent is usually necessary for the courts to consider an imitation a legal infringement of the original trademark. During 1929 the Standard Oil Company of Indiana utilized the results of a similar test, where pictures of various trade-marks were shown to students in the University of Chicago. The confusion between the original trademark "Red Crown" and the imitation "Red Hat" was considerably below 30 per cent, yet the court considered the results of the psychological test "significant" in decreeing that "Red Hat" was an infringement.

Some of the group and individual tests which have been mentioned utilize psychological technique. All interviewing endeavors to control conditions so as to eliminate bias. Investigators may not have to carry on so-called psychological tests, yet they should be acquainted with the general methods, and with the results which can be obtained. In the preceding table a relative confusion is shown in column one (Order) and an absolute confusion in column two (Percentage confusion). Sometimes both the relative and the absolute cannot be obtained, yet psychological methods give a correct answer so far as the data extend. The best container, trade-mark, inclosure, color, etc., of the group submitted can be found. The one limitation is that the really best package, for example, may not be in the group submitted. Care, however, makes this risk slight.

Test Selling.—Test selling occurs when a manufacturer tries out a new product or a new policy in a limited market. Care should be taken that the sample is representative. When the market (or several typical ones) has been selected, sufficient selling pressure is applied to obtain satisfactory distribution. The new product, or policy, is then watched, checked up on, modified, and revised until its success or failure in the sample market chosen is clearly determined. Upon this experience, decision is made as to whether to continue experimentation, to abandon, or to adopt the new product or policy.

The disadvantages of using salesmen as interviewers has been discussed (see Chapter VII). Interviewers can be used for selling, however, without encountering trouble.

Compensation should be a flat salary and not in any way a commission upon volume of sales. The ideal investigator, however, lacks usually certain characteristics which make a good salesman. Enthusiastic "boosters" seldom make good investigators. On the other hand, the field force will usually yield a few men who can conduct both test selling and investigation. If not, the investigators may accompany the regular salesmen, while the new product is being introduced, in order to get acquainted with the trade and with the local situation.

Trial Campaigns.—The trial advertising campaign is used to learn the best media, copy, illustrations, etc., for a particular product and purpose in a limited market area, before launching a larger campaign. With a carefully selected group of markets, various different illustrations, for example, are used with the same copy. A record of sales and inquiries is kept and the best illustration is eventually determined. Investigators are used to check up on window displays, outdoor advertising, and other media which are placed in public view. This type of checking the effectiveness of advertising has been somewhat neglected in the past but is now on the increase.

How Westinghouse Used a Tryout Market.—The Westinghouse Electric and Manufacturing Company brought out a new iron with a thermostatic disk automatic heat control which worked with a "click."[1] The company desired to test this product in a medium-sized city with urban and suburban population, finally deciding on Rochester. This city had good electrical service, with able jobbers and dealers in the electrical appliance line.

The merchandising department sent men to Rochester with irons and a carefully worked out newspaper and direct-mail campaign. A jobber was found who would agree to a quota of 1,000 irons in one month. With the start of dealer advertising, the jobber salesmen and the

[1] *Printers' Ink*, April 23, 1925, p. 49.

Westinghouse merchandising men obtained 90 per cent of the logical distribution quickly before consumer advertising began. A total of 1,250 irons was sold within the month, and several thousand more in surrounding territory soon afterward. All selling effort was then stopped for one year.

The first few hundred irons had cards inclosed with them. Purchasers were requested to record on these cards what feature of the new iron impressed them most. A convenient side-rest attachment was sent to those buyers who turned in a properly filled out card. It was soon found, as a result, that the "click" was the most impressive feature of the iron.

After a lapse of one year, representatives of the company were sent to Rochester to interview the purchasers, especially those who had filled out cards. This survey conclusively proved that the "click" was the most striking feature of the iron; so its name was changed to "Click-Iron." It was likewise discovered that the iron was the subject of much discussion among neighbors; therefore "over the back fence" conversational copy was adopted for the advertising which shortly followed. Distribution was expanded to cities such as New York, Buffalo, Syracuse, Cleveland, Pittsburgh, Chicago, etc., with consistent success.

The fact that "women talked it over" was also applied in merchandising the "Click-Iron." Dealers were given cardboard sheets upon which to record every buyer's name and the date of the purchase. The buyer was then given three coupons which had numbers referring to the blank where the purchaser's name was written. These coupons were worth a 25 cent discount if used by the friend of a purchaser to buy an iron within a certain time limit. A simple serial number arrangement on the dealer record sheet made calculations easy for both dealer and buyer. Each coupon had two selling points on it and every purchaser who had all three coupons turned in before the expiration of the time limit was given a free ironing-pad which retailed at $1.50 but cost the dealer only 75 cents. The total selling cost was thus 50 cents at most—a 25 cent discount for the coupon and a 25 cent bonus (one-third of a pad) to the consumer sending the new buyer in. There was thus no need for giving special commissions to clerks, etc., yet selling effort was kept up continually through this "endless chain" arrangement.

Rochester furnished the ideas behind the advertising and merchandising policies. These were tried in several additional cities, where they worked successfully. The test was then considered complete, with results that warranted attempting national distribution under these same policies.

PART FIVE

WORK OF THE CENTRAL OFFICE

Part Five describes the work done by the central office on a specific problem after the general program has been decided upon. This section describes the actual functions performed by the personnel of the home office, while Part Three presented its supervisory functions.

Chapter XIV explains how the questionnaire is created, and how it is tested to ascertain that it will successfully gather the desired material. In the next two chapters, editing and tabulating the returns, the drawing of conclusions from them, and the creation of a report based upon proved facts are described. Finally, in the last chapter, the methods used to check the validity of the work from beginning to end are presented.

CHAPTER XIV

PREPARATION OF QUESTIONNAIRES

THE questionnaire is used to seek information which is not more easily obtained in any other way. Data available from the company's records and from published sources must first be examined, to indicate what additional facts must be found.

Internal Situation Survey.—Market analysis, including the internal situation survey, is dealt with in Chapter III. Only one example of the value of an internal situation survey will be given here.

A clothing manufacturer sold his products through five hundred outlets located in forty-six states.[1] This appeared to be national distribution and a campaign in national magazines was being considered. A careful analysis of sales, however, showed that the manufacturer's chain of stores, which represented only 6 per cent of his outlets, accounted for 60 per cent of the sales volume. His franchised stores, representing only 4 per cent of the outlets, accounted for 25 per cent of the sales. Dealers at large, representing 90 per cent of the outlets, accounted for only 15 per cent of the sales volume. Analyzing the situation geographically, it was found that stores doing 90 per cent of the sales volume were located in a small number of cities of over 100,000 population. These cities were located in six states; so no real national distribution existed.

An internal situation survey showed that the problem

---

[1] "What a Sales Research Department Does," by S. I. Clark, Director of Sales Research, Lehn & Fink, Inc., in *Printers' Ink*, January 16, 1930, p. 152.

of this clothing manufacturer was entirely different from what he thought it to be. This is often the case and no field work can be efficiently done until the real facts needed are clearly marked out. Company records must be examined and company officials must be interviewed.

Bibliographical Work.—Many surveys have been conducted needlessly, since the information required was already available from a reputable source. More often, certain parts of the requisite data have already been collected. Therefore bibliographical research should be made before beginning field work.

Formulating the Questionnaire.—After determining what facts must be found in the field and the methods to be used, the questionnaire is drawn up. This is a complicated process because, on the one hand, complete data are essential to give the conclusions validity, while, on the other hand, the longer the questionnaire the harder and costlier it becomes to obtain satisfactory replies.

A plentiful collection of questions is first made, the responsible person including all which the latter and his associates can think of. These questions are then sorted and grouped until each group contains just one simple idea. A question for each simple idea or fact is then framed in the language which will appeal to the group of persons to be approached in the survey.

The following are good principles to follow in drawing up a questionnaire:

1. *Every question must be pertinent to the solution of the immediate problem.* Time is valuable to the people interested and the firm paying for the survey. Interviewers are likely to become discouraged if questionnaires are so long that it is difficult to obtain complete answers. Also, interviewers do poorer work and their morale is impaired when the answers to certain questions appear meaningless or inapplicable. They reason that, if one question is unimportant, all of them may be unimportant.

2. *Every question must have only one idea, clearly expressed.* If a question has two ideas one may remain unanswered. "Where do you buy canned soup? Why?" is a common type of double question. Two separate questions should be asked, "Where do you buy canned soup?" and "Why do you buy canned soup there?" Everything is to be gained by making the questions easy to answer.

Questions which are not clear bring vague answers. Ambiguous questions cause inapplicable answers. "Assuming that price is not a consideration, what type of house would you prefer to own?" is a question violating all of these rules. The primer form of question is always preferable.

3. *Facts alone should be asked.* Consumers and dealers often present opinions poorly, even though they may be able to give facts without trouble. If it is essential to have opinions, ask several short questions which require factual answers. Do not ask, "What, in your opinion, has been the success of X product locally?" but have several short questions starting with, "Do any of your friends use X product?" "Do your friends who use X product like it?" etc. The person's true opinion will thus be learned.

4. *Questions must not require mathematical calculations.* Except in cases where a percentage is 0 or 100, the person interviewed is more likely to make an error in calculating percentages than either the interviewer or the tabulator. Ask for data which will allow the percentage to be worked out later: "How often do you buy X brand of coffee?" "In what quantities do you buy X?" "What amount of coffee do you sell each week?"

5. *Questions must not suggest their answers.* This is the problem of the "leading question." If the first question asked a housewife is, "Do you use X soap?" the whole interview will be tinged by the fact that the housewife knows that you are particularly interested in that brand. Ordinarily it is better to ask, "What brands of soap do you

commonly use?" If X brand is not mentioned, it can easily be introduced into the conversation by saying, "I notice that you have not mentioned one or two popular brands. Have you ever tried X or Y soap?" Under unusual conditions, it may be desirable to ask what might be called a leading question. If information is desired from Ford owners alone, it will save time and money if the first question is, "Do you own a Ford?" A form such as, "You have your nails manicured by a professional manicurist, don't you?" is, however, always unpardonable. The question should not give the person interviewed a clue to the answer expected.

6. *Personal questions must be avoided.* A housewife will very seldom state the income of her husband. If she does, it is likely to be exaggerated. If a personal question is asked early in the interview, the call is likely to end abruptly. If necessary to ask personal questions, do so at the end of the interview.

7. *Impossible questions must not be asked.* "Where have you seen advertisements of Y?" "Were you influenced in buying an X vacuum cleaner by the advertising of the X company?" People cannot answer such questions satisfactorily. Advertisements are "seen" in media where they never appeared. Price may have been the thing that sold the X vacuum cleaner, but the question focuses attention on advertising and the answers are undependable.

8. *All essential questions must be included.* If the fact which a question brings forth is essential, do not omit the question. The longer the questionnaire, the more difficult and expensive the survey, yet the results are unreliable unless all of the vital facts are ascertained. Ten questions may be too many for one survey and two hundred too few for another, but needless questions should never be included because their answers might be "interesting."

Testing the Questionnaire.—When a preliminary questionnaire has been drawn up, it should be tried out.

WOOLEN BLANKET SURVEY

CONSUMER QUESTIONNAIRE

1. How many beds have you in your home?

Single.......... Three-quarter.......... Double..........

2. How many, and what makes of blankets have you?

Brand	(Check 1)				(Check 1)				
Where Possible	Light	Med.	Heavy	Cotton Mix	Single	Double	Size	Price or	Was it a Gift?
....	...	...	...	...	...	...	...	...	...
....	...	...	...	...	...	...	...	...	...
....	...	...	...	...	...	...	...	...	...
....	...	...	...	...	...	...	...	...	...
....	...	...	...	...	...	...	...	...	...
....	...	...	...	...	...	...	...	...	...
....	...	...	...	...	...	...	...	...	...

If any of the prices were sale or mark-down prices, please check (X) beside price.

3. Which brand do you prefer?.......... Why?..........

4. What do you think a fair price for a colored wool blanket? Single $..... Double $.....

What do you think a fair price for a white wool blanket? Single $..... Double $.....

5. Have you ever given blankets as gifts? Yes..... No..... What price paid? Single $..... Double $.....

If so, which brands..........

6. Which do you prefer?

Single blankets.......... Double blankets..........

Why?..........

FIG. 48A

A portion of a questionnaire, showing the changes caused by testing. A is the preliminary form, B is the final form.

Associates, stenographers, members of the family, or similar people will do for this first test. Revision will be found necessary; questions will be misunderstood or ambiguous; those which seemed important will be shown to be trivial, etc. When this revision is completed, have investigators make a small number of interviews. A further revision will then be found necessary. No more testing may be required, but the questionnaire should never go out as a finished product until it has stood a good field test. Fig. 48, A and B, pages 181 and 183 show the same questionnaire before and after actual field testing. The Albert P. Hill Company of Pittsburgh has found that testing questionnaires in the field on a small scale provides a quick and inexpensive way to determine:

1. Whether the questionnaire provides the information desired.
2. Whether the information is obtained in the manner best suited for tabulation and analysis.
3. Whether the interviewer has grasped the important factors to be developed.
4. Whether or not there are new angles to the subject which ought to be developed in the field investigation.

As a final test, it is again desirable to apply the eight principles stated on pages 178, 179, 180. For example, 75 per cent of the replies are "Yes" and 25 per cent "No." If such a tabulation (or its reverse) will be of assistance in solving the problem, leave the question in; if not, omit it. Another check is to make a hypothetical tabulation for all of the questions in order to see whether such data will furnish an answer to the problem to be solved.

Organizing the Questionnaire.—When the subject-matter and general form of the questionnaire have been determined, there are certain rules which, if followed, make responses better and easier to obtain. These are:

1. Simple questionnaires are better than complex ones.
2. Short questionnaires are better than long ones.

3. Brief answers are easier to get and are more dependable.
4. Where "Yes" and "No" are printed, include a "Don't

WOOLEN BLANKET SURVEY

CONSUMER QUESTIONNAIRE

1. How many, and what makes of blankets have you?

No.		Brands	Wool	(Check 1) Cotton Mix	Cotton	Single	(Check 1) Pair
1	3	North Star	14-1 ✓	14-2	14-3	14-1 ✓	14-5
2		Esmond	15-1	15-2	15-3	15-4	15-5
3	1	Kenwood	16-1 ✓	16-2	16-3	16-4 ✓	16-5
4		St. Mary's	17-1	17-2	17-3	17-4	17-5
5	2	Nashua	18-1	18-2 ✓	18-3	18-4	18-5 ✓
6		Chatham	19-1	19-2	19-3	19-4	19-5
7		Old Town	20-1	20-2	20-3	20-4	20-5
8		Mariposa	21-1	21-2	21-3	21-4	21-5
9		Lady Seymour	22-1	22-2	22-3	22-4	22-5
10		Pendleton	23-1	23-2	23-3	23-4	23-5
11		Oregon City	24-1	24-2 ✓	24-3	24-4	24-5
12	3	Don't know	25-1	25-2 ✓	25-3	25-4 3	25-5 2
13		All others	26-1	26-2	26-3	26-4	26-5

2. How many blankets (white) have you? 27 —

How many colored blankets have you? 28 4

How many reversible blankets have you? 29 2

How many comforters have you? 30 2

How many quilts have you? 31 —

How many throws have you? 32 —

3. How many beds have you? Total: 33 3

Beds

Single 34-1   Three-quarter 34-2 2   Double 34-3

4. Do you vary the weight of blankets according to seasons by using:

    1. Different weight of blankets 35-1

        or

    2. By varying the number of blankets 35-2 ✓

FIG. 48B

know." It is as important to measure ignorance as knowledge.
5. Always have a space of ample size for comments, remarks, and opinions. The meat of the survey may be in such extra material.

6. Always allow sufficient space for the desired information and for any necessary explanatory notes. If there is no convenient space, explanations are often omitted.

7. Important questions should come first while the prospect is fresh. If you want to obtain advertising appeals, begin with reasons for the purchase of the article.

8. Related questions should come together. If one question is used to check the answer to a preceding one, they may be separated, but this checking device should not be obvious.

9. A natural conversational order for the questions is best. A logical order is necessary.

10. Positive questions are better than negative ones.

11. If possible, be sure to give the person interviewed a reason why he should answer the questions.

12. The classification part of the questionnaire—locality, income group, occupation—must be complete.

Types of Questionnaires.—Questionnaires are divided into three types: 1. Interviewing questionnaires, directed at the person interviewed, the investigator asking the questions exactly as they are written on the questionnaire blank. 2. Interviewing questionnaires directed at the investigator who formulates his own approach for obtaining satisfactory answers to the written questions. 3. Mail questionnaires which are sent to selected persons in the hope that they will fill in the answers and return the questionnaires.

Personal Interview Questionnaires.—In the case of consumer surveys, the questionnaire is frequently worded so that the interviewer need only ask the written questions. When unskilled investigators are used to interview relatively unintelligent persons, the questions are always asked as they appear on the questionnaire. This procedure tends to obtain uniform results of a factual nature. Although comments will be obtained, primary emphasis is laid upon the facts asked for in the questions. Fig. 49, on page 185, shows a questionnaire of this type.

When local color and peculiarities are desired, questions

aimed at the investigator are frequently used. If executives
are to be approached, this plan is also best. Uniform results
are difficult to obtain, since each investigator will work
out a different method of approach. If the questionnaire,

Name ....

Street ....Number ....

Check Regular Paid Subscriptions Only:

Dispatch ....Journal ....

News ....Times Herald................

If limited to one paper which one would you prefer?........

Residence ....Apartment..............

Owner ....Renter ....

If apartment dweller how long in present location?.........

AA.........A.........B.........C.........D.........

Occupation ....

Remarks ....

....

Name of Investigator.................................

District ....Date ....

FIG. 49
A simple factual questionnaire.

however, asks for certain definite facts, these will be forthcoming in tabulatable form. The comments are likely to
be copious and valuable, especially since the questionnaires
can indicate materials which, while not absolutely essential,
may be very desirable (see Fig. 50 on page 186). For good
results, only skilled investigators of high quality should be
used with this type of questionnaire.

Mail Questionnaires.—The mail questionnaire is somewhat different from that for the personal interview. There will be no interviewer present to explain anything to the

---

When starting the interview, show the sample to the person with whom you talk. Then secure as much information as you can regarding the following questions:

1. The general market possibilities for this product.
2. Is there a possibility in the export market?
3. What do you think of the price?
4. How does it turn over?
5. Does it repeat?
6. What type of women buy it?
7. What do you think of the name?
8. What suggestions have you about advertising and selling methods?
9. What are this product's particular
   (a) advantages
   (b) disadvantages
10. Have you any idea of how it could be improved?
11. How does it compare?
    (a) Is it superior?
    (b) Is it inferior?

Do not limit yourself to this outline. We wish you to discuss the subject as exhaustively as possible with the person you interview. We also would like you to write a very detailed report for each interview on the topics outlined above.

FIG. 50

Questionnaire which asks the investigator questions and permits him to acquire this information by any technique he sees fit to use. Copious comments are likely when this method is used

person who is to answer the questions. The whole contact will be through the written word. As a result, there are certain additional principles which apply to the use of the mail questionnaire.

1. *Mail questionnaires must be short.* Ten questions are a maximum beyond which additional ones greatly cut down returns. Five questions are better.

2. *"Yes" and "No" or "Check" answers bring the best results.* Questions requiring long answers will usually be

| M 2 3537 2 30 |
| MRS CLINT MARRETT |
| WEBB CITY MO |
| 3 25 209663 |

1. Please mark a cross (x) in the space opposite the kind of stove you use for cooking.	Wood		3. How soon do you expect to buy another cooking stove?	1 year	
	Coal	X		2 years	X
	Kerosene			3 years	
	Gasoline			4 or more	
	Gas				
	Electric				
2. What kind of a stove do you expect to buy next?	Wood		4. In what town do you expect to buy your next stove?		
	Coal		*Name of Town* Webb City		
	Kerosene	X			
	Gasoline		5. Do you live on a farm? Yes		
	Gas				
	Electric				

FIG. 51

A mail questionnaire reproduced upon a postcard

left blank. The questions must be such that a short answer can be easily made.

3. *The first question must be interesting.* The people who receive the questionnaire must be interested and impressed by it or the responses will be few.

4. *The type of answer desired must be indicated.* Give

direct indications of the answer desired in parentheses—
make of car, brand name, number of pounds, etc.

5. *Select the mailing list carefully.* Know what classes
of people are on the mailing list because those who do not
answer may be as important as those who reply.

6. *Distinguish between classifications on the questionnaire.* This may be done by using one color of paper for
the high-income group, a second color for the moderate-
income group, etc. Numbering systems also are used.

7. *Inclose a stamped and addressed envelope.* This will
usually cut down the cost per return.

8. *A dummy company* may be used for sending out the
questionnaires. Unbiased results are more likely if the organization for whose benefit the information is being
obtained is unknown.

9. *Always give the person addressed a reason for answering.* Even if the questionnaire is on a postcard, the
prospective respondent must be "sold" on the idea of answering the questions (see Fig. 51 on page 187).

The U. S. Department of Agriculture has found that
returns from mail questionnaires are increased by having
them printed, this increase being more than sufficient to
compensate for the extra expense involved. Color of paper
has also been found important. Yellow paper was found to
draw best, and pink second best, while the dark colors gave
lower returns. If questionnaires are sent repeatedly to the
same people on the same colored paper, the response gradually decreases. Alternating between pink and yellow paper
has given good results. The department has also learned
that the more intelligent and better educated farmers respond more readily to mail questionnaires, and that the
information which is given is surprisingly accurate.

The Mail Questionnaire Letter.—A one-page letter
commonly accompanies the mail questionnaire. An example
of this is shown in Fig. 52 on page 189. In a few cases, the
questionnaire and letter are on the same sheet or card.

PERCIVAL WHITE
INCORPORATED
MARKETING COUNSELORS
25 WEST 45TH STREET
NEW YORK
CABLES: DEODIKKA

September 4, 1930

Mr. F. L. Hastings,
9 Ridgefield Place,
Hastings, N. Y.

Dear Sir:

We are making a study of various kinds of roof-
ing materials, the reasons why architects specify
slate and tile, and how the tile manufacturers can
extend a more helpful service to architects.

Rather than interrupt you by seeking a personal
interview during business hours, we are taking the
liberty of asking if you will be kind enough to answer the questions on the attached form and return
it in the enclosed stamped envelope.

Please let us assure you that "Strictly Confidential" at the top of the blank means exactly what it
says. Your name and your opinions will not be disclosed to others,- we are interested only in gathering and compiling factual data on the subject.

We are preparing a brief resumé of the opinions
of prominent architects and qualified observers on
trends in styles of architecture. If you would care
for a complimentary copy, when ready, we shall be glad
to send it.

Thank you most cordially for your valuable cooperation and assistance.

Yours faithfully,

Percival White

FIG. 52

A one-page letter which accompanied a mail questionnaire and
brought excellent results

The letter must "sell" the idea of filling out and returning the questionnaire. The letter is as important as the questionnaire. The Department of Agriculture has found that successful letters consist of:

1. An appropriate salutation or caption.
2. An interesting approach.
3. A first paragraph that will gain attention.
4. Material that will hold interest; create realization of the seriousness of the problem; arouse a desire for remedy; make a favorable impression; cause a decision to act.
5. A closing statement that will encourage prompt action.

Some rules for composing successful mail questionnaire letters have been formulated by Jean F. Carroll, Director, Bureau of Market Analysis of the Meredith Publishing Company. Mr. Carroll states that a letter must be:

1. Interesting. The letter should be original.
2. Clearly understood. There must be no doubt as to the information wanted and why.
3. Tactful. The language must cause no offense.
4. Sincere. The person questioned must be impressed.
5. Suited to the type of person questioned. The language must be that used by the class of people who receive the letter.
6. Suited to the type of information wanted. A request for personal information must be handled so as not to give the impression of curiosity.
7. Courteous. The person addressed is being asked a favor which will be gratefully received.
8. Confidential. All information received will be considered confidential. If used separately, as in quoting it, the name of the person from whom it was received will be omitted.

Inducements to Reply.—Sometimes, in addition to the favor of a reply which is asked, an inducement is offered in an endeavor to get larger returns. Often a summary of the results is promised. In the case of housewives, recipe

J. R. Watkins Co.,
Winona, Minn.

Gentlemen:

Would you be so kind as to do a small favor for a fellow business man who has a hard problem in front of him right now?

This fellow business man is a client of ours. His firm is the outstanding leader in their industry in the United States. They are rated AAA-1 and their volume of business runs into many millions.

You have been selected as a representative concern in your line, whose opinions our client would like to have. We trust the chief executive of your business will be willing to take just a few seconds to help another big business executive solve a difficult problem in these days of fierce competition.

Eight questions are enclosed herewith, which can be answered practically "yes" or "no." Your first natural reactions, without any detailed study of the questions, is the thing our client seeks.

All you have to do is to check the questionnaire and enclose in the stamped and addressed envelope herewith. You don't even have to sign your name. But you can, of course, if you wish.

We hope you will be disposed to grant our client this courtesy, and if we or our client can reciprocate in any way whatsoever, we will be only too glad to do so.

If you would be interested in a digest of all the answers to this questionnaire when it is finished, we would be very glad to send you a copy.

Thanking you in advance for your kindness,

Yours sincerely,

CHAPPELOW ADVERTISING COMPANY,

B. E. CHAPPELOW,
President.

FIG. 53

This mail questionnaire letter offers a small inducement for returning the filled-in questionnaire. It is surprising how many people are interested in a digest of current information

LELIA WELLES
247 PARK AVENUE
NEW YORK CITY

May 11, 1926

To the
Lady of the House

Dear Madam:-

Would you be astonished to learn that
there are at least 60 known household uses for
cheesecloth ?

It has been suggested that some housewives may have discovered new and unfamiliar
uses for this inexpensive product that should
be brought to the attention of all women.

In an effort, therefore, to determine
the full extent of these uses, both new and old,
to which cheesecloth is put in the household, I
am writing you and certain other ladies whose
opinions would be of value.

Whether you use cheesecloth or not, I
would greatly appreciate your answering as many
questions on the accompanying page as you can.
Your cooperation will be of distinct service to
one of America's oldest industries in the interest of which this investigation is being made.
Incidentally, your reply will benefit many thou-
sands of women.

A stamped and addressed envelope is enclosed for your convenience. Won't you return
the questionnaire as soon as possible ?

It is not necessary for you to sign your
name unless you desire me to send you an attractive booklet suggesting the many ways in which
you can use cheesecloth.

Sincerely yours,

Lelia Welles

JH

1. Do you or your family use cheesecloth?

    Yes....................   No.....................

2. (a) If you do, for what purposes is it used?

    ....
    ....
    ....
    ....

    (b) If you do not, why do you not use it?

    .....:..
    ....
    ....

3. State the kind of store in which you purchase each of the follow-
    ing articles?   (For example: Department, Dry Goods, Furniture,
    Grocery, Hardware or Drug Store.)

    NOTE: If you do not use any of these articles, kindly write "Do
    not use" after such articles.

                                        Kind of Store

    Cleansing Powders   ....
    Kitchen Soap   ....
    Toilet Soap   ....
    Floor Wax   ....
    Furniture Polish   ....
    Metal Polish   ....
    Silver Polish   ....
    Preserve Jars   ....

4. In what kind of a store do you now purchase cheesecloth?

    ....

5. Would it be convenient for you to be able to purchase cheese-
    cloth in—
                    (In answering this question check "Yes" or "No" for each store.)

    Furniture Stores   Yes.............   No.............
    Grocery Stores   Yes.............   No.............
    Hardware Stores   Yes.............   No.............
    Drug Stores   Yes.............   No.............

D

FIG. 54

This mail questionnaire letter offers a small inducement (a booklet) for returning the questionnaire properly filled in

booklets are frequently given as a reward for filling out the questionnaire. If a reward is offered, it should be both useful and inexpensive. It must be useful so as to offer an incentive for getting it, yet inexpensive enough that the incentive is not so great as to encourage false answers. Figs. 53, 54 on pages 191, 192 and 193 illustrate this.

CHAPTER XV

TABULATING RETURNS

COMPLETED questionnaires begin to come in from the field soon after the survey starts. These must be checked at once so that any necessary suggestions can be immediately sent to the investigators. Such checking of returns is called editing and is necessary to get the questionnaires into comparable form.

Editing.—An experienced research man must be in charge of the editing. He should be familiar with the subject of the investigation and of a very observing nature. Conservatism is necessary, or the editing may give a bias to the whole survey. Clerks should never be used except to mark errors which will later be handled by the editor.

Reports are edited for consistency, completeness, accuracy, and probability. All of the editing should be checked by a second person. Changes are sometimes made in the reports, but the original is never erased. The assumption is that the report is true until proved false. Some editing rules follow:

1. All editing must be in red ink and the original must never be erased.
2. No answers should be changed without sufficient justification obtained from the data given in other answers.
3. Obvious answers should be supplied. In a mail questionnaire, "Do you own an automobile?" may be left blank, while "What make of automobile do you own?" may be answered. The answer to the second question is also the answer to the first.
4. Extremely doubtful answers should be discarded. For

example, it is hardly probable that a family of four would consume five hundred cans of baked beans in a year.

5. Changes made for consistency should always be carefully examined. Two contradictory answers should both be thrown out unless the answers to other questions indicate which of the two is correct. When several answers are contradictory, throw out the questionnaire.

6. When answers are in different units of measurement these should be reduced to a common unit.

7. When opinions or comments occur, the editor may arbitrarily classify these for tabulation.

Explanations and comments must be examined by the editor. These may open a new approach to the problem or explain a variation in facts in different localities. Interviewers should be immediately informed about any defects in their completed questionnaires and should be requested to ask additional questions if the early returns indicate the need of doing so.

Methods of Tabulation.—Tabulation can be done either by hand or by machine. If the questionnaire is long and a great number of reports are received, machine tabulation is most economical. If many cross analyses are wanted, the tabulating machine is also to be preferred. If the questionnaire is short and simple, hand tabulation may be more economical. A very interesting comparison of these two methods is given by the Bureau of Agricultural Economics of the U. S. Department of Agriculture:

It is advisable to use mechanical tabulation when the number of cases to be tabulated is large and when a considerable number of sub-sortings or cross tabulations is wanted. It is especially economical to use a machine for tabulating when data of the same type are brought in at frequent intervals so that a definite system of coding can be standardized and learned by the clerks.

An important disadvantage of machine tabulation is the

large number of errors made in the punching of cards, especially when this punching is done by clerks who are not familiar with the project. Many who have used machines have come to the conclusion that they can be safely used only when the schedules have been closely edited, so that they are

REASONS FOR PREFERENCE
WOMEN

	Lucky Strike	Chester-field	Camel	Old Gold	Tarey-ton	Marl-boro	No Brand	Others	Total
Don't irritate throat..	10	3	1	1		1			16
First by advertising...	3	1		1					5
Prove satisfactory by trial.............	6	1	4	1					12
Individual taste......	2								2
Pleasant taste.......	6	1	3		1			1	12
Best suited to use....	3	1	2	1				1	8
Campaign against candy...........	1								1
Husband smokes them	5	1	8					1	15
Thrilling taste—quiets nerves...........	1		1						2
Habit.............	3		3					1	7
Not too strong—mild.	3	1			2			1	7
Don't cause headache.	1	2							3
Don't bite tongue....		2	1					2	5
Taken fancy to them..		1							1
Started with........		1	3						4
Just preference......	2		1	1					4
Don't know why.....			1						1
Others make me cough			2						2
Like the tip........					2	3		2	7
Better quality.......		1						1	2
All satisfactory.....							2		2
No preferences......							3		3
Satisfying..........			1						1
Personal taste.......	1								1
Packed solid........			1						1
No after taste.......		1							1
Self-lighting........								1	1
Slow-smoke........								1	1
	47	16	31	7	5	4	5	12	127

FIG. 55
An example of recording facts by hand tabulation

fool-proof, and that even then all punchings must be supervised very carefully. There is the further difficulty that errors made in the punching are very difficult to locate.

In studies which lend themselves to machine methods because of the size or the large number of sortings, the cost can frequently be reduced by as much as one-third. The saving in time is really in the sorting.

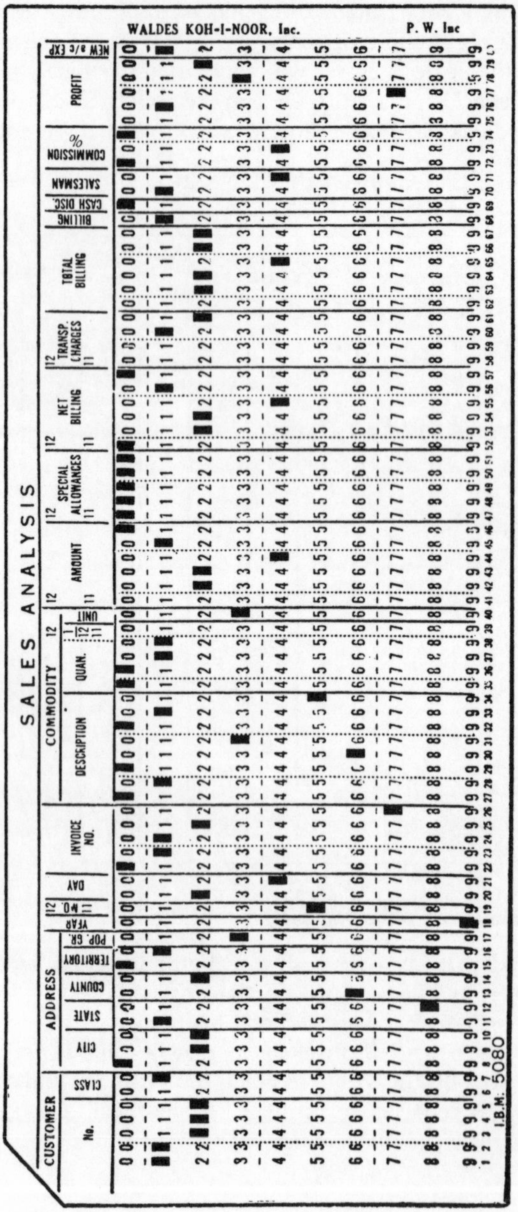

FIG. 56

Hollerith tabulating card with punched holes. Each hole represents a certain definite answer occurring in the questionnaire

The principles of hand and machine tabulation are the same. Machine tabulation will be outlined. Hand tabulation ordinarily consists of recording the facts on tally sheets (see Fig. 55 on page 197) instead of punched cards, the data being in less mobile form, since all of the reports must be again gone over if some unexpected type of analysis becomes necessary.

Coding.—The Hollerith tabulating card (see Fig. 56 on page 198) is standard and consists of eighty vertical columns with ten figures in each (0 to 9). Each questionnaire is assigned a card. Each item on the questionnaire is assigned some definite figure in a certain column. A common method is to assign a vertical column to each question and a number to each probable answer. For example, "What brand of cigarettes do you smoke?" may be assigned column three and Brand A space zero, Brand B space one, etc. Where the possible answers are more than ten, two columns may be used for a question, if the questionnaire is long, two cards may be necessary for each return.

When the completed questionnaires have been edited, the appropriate code symbols are entered beside each tabulation unit of the questionnaire. If precoding has taken place this will be already done. The correct symbols are then transferred to cards by means of punching machines, a small hole in the appropriate position representing each symbol.

Precoding.—A code may be made for a questionnaire after the completed returns have come in from the field. It is advisable, however, to prepare the code in advance and, if possible, have the code symbols already on the questionnaire, except in the case of mail questionnaires, where the code symbols might confuse the respondent. Precoded questionnaires are shown in Figs. 57, 58 on pages 200, 201, 202 and 203.

Precoding has become standard practice because:

1. It forces unusually careful and minute analysis of the questions and the applicability of their answers.
2. Investigators can mark appropriate symbols and economize on time.

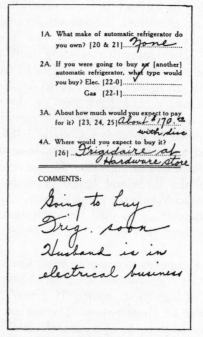

FIG. 57
An example of a precoded questionnaire

3. Reports may be tabulated as they come in from the field. This partial tabulation may show a need for additional information, etc.
4. It reduces cost due to the above.

Sampling.—When the questionnaire has been written and tested, the question, "How many interviews are necessary to make our results reliable?" has yet to be answered. Precoding and advance analysis of returns are the first

R. O. EASTMAN, *INCORPORATED*
7016 EUCLID AVENUE, CLEVELAND, OHIO

ENTERED

EDITED

No.

REPORTER:

SURVEY: No. 1641   8921   CODED   DATE _____

A. CLASSIFICATION

1. Name:
   ....
   ....

2. Address:
   ....

3. District: (x)
A.	60
B.	61
C.	62
D.	63
E.	64
F.	65
G.	66
H.	67
I.	68
J.	69
K.	6X
L.	70
M.	71
N.	72
O.	73
P.	74
Q.	75
R.	76

SECTION.........

4. Vocation of self or head of family: (x)
Executive	80
Professional	81
Merchant	82
Sub-executive	83
Salesman	84
Public service	85
Clerical	86
Skilled labor	87
Unskilled labor	88
Widow or independent income	89
Miscellaneous	8X

5. Number in household: (xd)
   9–

6. Approximate age: (xi)
Under 20	100
20 to 30	101
30 to 40	102
40 to 50	103
Over 50	104
	†

7. Income class: (xi)
Under $1,000 ($40)	105
$1,000 to $4,000 ($40–$80)	106
$4,000 to $6,000 ($80–$120)	107
$6,000 to $10,000 ($120–$200)	108
Over $10,000	109
Unable to estimate	10X

8. Class of home: (xi)
A.	110
B.	111
C.	112
D.	113

9. Kind of home: (x)
Home owned	†
Rented (single or double)	115
Rented (apartment)	116

10. Length of residence in greater Pittsburg: (x)
Native	117
Less than 3 years	118
3 to 10 years	119
Over 10 years	11X

11. Automobile:
    Name: (x).................. 12..
    None:...................x 13..
    Class: (x)
None	140
A.	141
B.	142
C.	143

---

12. Home equipment: (x)
	Yes	No
Telephone	150	160
Gas	151	161
Electricity	152	162
Elec. Wash. Machine	153	163
Elec. Refrigerator	154	164
Vacuum Sweeper	155	165
Radio	156	166
Phonograph	157	167
Piano	158	168

B. TRADING HABITS

13. Does party maintain charge accounts at downtown stores: (x)
Yes	16X
No	16Y

14. What downtown stores patronized regularly: (xf)
    (Reporter ask specifically on each group)

    DEPARTMENT STORES:
None	170
Boggs & Buhl	171
Gimbel's	172
Frank & Seder	173
Campbell's	174
Joseph Horne Co.	175
Kaufmann's	176
Lewin-Neiman Co.	177
McCreery & Co.	178
Rosenbaum's	179
Harris Dept. Store	17X

    GROCERY STORES:
None	180
Atlantic & Pac. Tea Co.	181
P. H. Butler Co.	182
Donahoe's	183
McCann & Co.	184
Kroger's	185

    MUSICAL INSTRUMENTS:
None	186
S. Hamilton & Co.	187
Volkwein Bros.	188
Wurlitzer's	189
W. F. Frederick Piano Co.	18X
Lechner & Schoenberger	18Y
C. C. Mellor Co.	190
Schroeder Piano Co.	191

    WOMEN'S WEAR STORES:
None	192
Bedell	193
Grabowsky	†
Kaufmann Looby Co.	195
Meyer-Jonasson Co.	196
Oppenheim-Collins Co.	197

    MEN'S STORES:
None	198
Bennett	199
Browning-King	19X
Richman's	19Y
George M. Wilson	200

    SHOE STORES:
None	201
Book	202
Kirby	203
Hanan	204
Stetson Shop	205
Van Deventer	206
Verner	207
Walk-Over	208
Wise	209

JEWELRY STORES:
None	210
Louis DeRoy & Bro.	211
S. H. DeRoy & Co.	212
Grogan Co.	213
Hardy & Hayes	214
Kappel's	215
Loftis Bros.	216
John M. Roberts & Son	217
Terheyden & Co.	218
Unger	219
Wilken	21X

FURNITURE STORES:
None	220
Dauler-Close	221
Friend's	222
Hahn Furniture Co.	223
May Stern & Co.	224
Pickering	225
Select Furniture Corp.	226
The Clearance	227
Spear's	228
Taylor Bros.	229

DRUG STORES:
None	230
Liggett's	231
May's	232
McCulloch's	233
Boreman's	234

15. On what day, or days, last week did you go downtown for shopping: (x)
None	240
Monday	241
Tuesday	242
Wednesday	243
Thursday	244
Friday	245
Saturday	246
	†

C. NEWSPAPERS READ

16. How many Pittsburgh DAILY newspapers received in the home regularly or frequently (more than half of the time): (xd)
None	247
One	248
Two	249
Three	24X

17. Which Pittsburg papers received in this home regularly or frequently: (b)
Press daily	250
Sun-Telegraph daily	251
Post-Gazette daily	252
Press Sunday	253
Sun-Telegraph Sunday	254
None	255

18. Which Pittsburgh daily papers were read regularly or frequently before the consolidation August, 1927: (b)
Press	260
Chronicle-Telegraph	261
Sun	262
Post	263
Gazette-Times	264
None	265
Not remembered	26d

19. Comparison of papers now read regularly or frequently IN PLACE OF any one of those previously read (including Press):
    a. Press in place of Chronicle-Telegraph: (x) NA
Liked better	271
Not liked as well	272
No difference	273
	†

Page 2

b. Press in place of Sun: (a) NA...	274
Liked better................	275
Not liked as well................	276
No difference................	277
c. Sun-Telegraph in place of Chron-	
icle-Telegraph: (a) NA.............	278
Liked better................	279
Not liked as well................	27X
No difference................	27Y
d. Sun-Telegraph in place of Sun:	
(a) NA................	280
Liked better................	281
Not liked as well................	282
No difference................	283
e. Sun-Telegraph in place of Press:	†
(a) NA................	284
Liked better................	285
Not liked as well................	286
No difference................	287
f. Post-Gazette in place of Post:	†
(a) NA................	288
Liked better................	289
Not liked as well................	28X
No difference................	28Y
g. Post-Gazette in place of Gazette-	
Times: (a) NA................	290
Liked better................	291
Not liked as well................	292
No difference................	293
20. If party could have only one week-day	†
paper, which would he choose: (ad)	†
NA................	294
Press................	295
Sun-Telegraph................	296
Post-Gazette................	297
No choice................	298
21. Why: (Give reasons, or reasons, fully):	
(bky)	
	30..
	31..
22. In which paper (including Sunday)	
would party be most likely to see a	
certain advertisement which ran in all	
papers: (a)	
Press daily................	320
Sun-Telegraph daily................	321
Post-Gazette daily................	322
Press Sunday................	323
Sun-Telegraph Sunday................	324
No opinion................	325
23. If going shopping does she make it a	
point to look over the advertisements	
of the various stores first: (a)	
Always................	330
Frequently................	331
Occasionally................	332
Seldom................	333
Never................	334
24. Which paper (including Sundays) is	
she most likely to consult for this	
purpose: (haf)	
NA................	340
Press daily................	341
Sun-Telegraph daily................	342
Post-Gazette daily................	343
Press Sunday................	344
Sun-Telegraph Sunday................	345
No preference................	346
25. Which daily paper would party use or	†
consult for classified (or want) adver-	†
tising: (af) NA................	347
Press................	348
Sun-Telegraph................	349
Post-Gazette................	34X
No preference................	34Y
26. Why: (bky)	
	35..
	36..
CARD 1........ X	**451**

Section D:

PRESS DAILY

1. How received in this home: (r)	
Home delivered................	301
Bought................	302
Regularly................	303
Frequently (more than half the time)...	304
Occasionally................	305
In past but discontinued................	306
Never................	307
2. If received regularly or frequently,	
for how long has it been received: (adh)	
................years................	31..
................months................	32..
3. Number of regular readers: (d)	
Men................	33..
Women................	34..
Children (under 14)................	35..
Total................	36..
4. Who reads it the most: (a)	
Man or men................	371
Woman or Women................	372
Children................	373
All about equally................	374
5. What features of this paper are liked	
the best: (bf)	
General News................	380
Local news................	381
Outside news................	382
Advertising................	383
Women's page................	384
Society................	385
Stocks................	386
Sports................	387
Drama, Movies, Music................	388
Comics................	389
Fiction................	38x
Editorial................	390
Radio................	391
Politics................	392
Tracy's Column................	393
Pittsburgh Day by Day—Harper...	394
In New York—Swan................	395
Dorothy Dix Letter Box................	396
It Seems to Me—Heywood Broun...	397
Dr. Fishbein's Medical Talks........	398
Letters from Readers................	399
Questions and Answers................	39x
Other features (p)................	40..
6. Double check (in Q. 5) the ONE fea-	
ture of GREATEST interest: (a)	
....	41..
....	42..
....	43..
CARD 2........ X	**452**

Section D:

PRESS SUNDAY

1. How received in this home: (r)	
Home delivered................	301
Bought................	302
Regularly................	303
Frequently (more than half the time)...	304
Occasionally................	305
In past but discontinued................	306
Never................	307
2. If received regularly or frequently,	
for how long has it been received: (adh)	
................years................	31..
................months................	32..
3. Number of regular readers: (d)	
Men................	33..
Women................	34..
Children (under 14)................	35..
Total................	36..
4. Who reads it the most: (a)	
Man or men................	371
Woman or women................	372
Children................	373
All about equally................	374
5. What features of this paper are liked	
the best: (bf)	
General News................	380
Local news................	381
Outside news................	382
Advertising................	383
Women's page................	384
Society................	385
Stocks................	386
Sports................	387
Drama, Movies, Music................	388
Comics................	389
Fiction................	38x
Editorial................	390
Radio................	391
Politics................	392
Tracy's Column................	393
Pittsburgh Day by Day—Harper...	394
In New York—Swan................	395
Dorothy Dix Letter Box................	396
It Seems to Me—Heywood Broun...	397
Dr. Fishbein's Medical Talks........	398
Letters from Readers................	399
Questions and Answers................	39x
Rotogravure................	400
Magazine section................	401
Automobile section................	402
Real Estate News................	403
Fraternal News................	404
School news................	405
Other features (p)................	40..
6. Double check (in Q.5) the ONE fea-	
ture of GREATEST interest: (a)	
....	41..
....	42..
....	43..
CARD 3........ X	**453**

Page 3

Section D: SUN-TELEGRAPH DAILY		Section D: SUN-TELEGRAPH SUNDAY		Section D: POST-GAZETTE DAILY	
1. How received in this home: (r)		1. How received in this home: (r)		1. How received in this home: (r)	
Home delivered	301	Home delivered	301	Home delivered	301
Bought	302	Bought	302	Bought	302
Regularly	303	Regularly	303	Regularly	303
Frequently (more than half the time)	304	Frequently (more than half the time)	304	Frequently (more than half the time)	304
Occasionally	305	Occasionally	305	Occasionally	305
In past but discontinued	306	In past but discontinued	306	In past but discontinued	306
Never	307	Never	307	Never	307
2. If received regularly or frequently, for how long has it been received: (adh)		2. If received regularly or frequently, for how long has it been received: (adh)		2. If received regularly or frequently, for how long has it been received: (adh)	
..........years..........	31..	..........years..........	31..	..........years..........	31..
..........months..........	32..	..........months..........	32..	..........months..........	32..
3. Number of regular readers: (d)		3. Number of regular readers: (d)		3. Number of regular readers: (d)	
Men	33..	Men	33..	Men	33..
Women	34..	Women	34..	Women	34..
Children (under 14)	35..	Children (under 14)	35..	Children (under 14)	35..
Total	36..	Total	36..	Total	36..
4. Who reads it the most: (a)		4. Who reads it the most: (a)		4. Who reads it the most: (a)	
Man or men	371	Man or men	371	Man or men	371
Woman or women	372	Woman or women	372	Woman or women	372
Children	373	Children	373	Children	373
All about equally	374	All about equally	374	All about equally	374
5. What features of this paper are liked the best: (bf)		5. What features of this paper are liked the best: (bf)		5. What features of this paper are liked the best: (bf)	
General News	380	General news	380	General news	380
Local news	381	Local news	381	Local news	381
Outside news	382	Outside news	382	Outside news	382
Advertising	383	Advertising	383	Advertising	383
Women's page	384	Women's page	384	Women's page	384
Society	385	Society	385	Society	385
Stocks	386	Stocks	386	Stocks	386
Sports	387	Sports	387	Sports	387
Drama, Movies, Music	388	Drama, Movies, Music	388	Drama, Movies, Music	388
Comics	389	Comics	389	Comics	389
Fiction	38x	Fiction	38x	Fiction	38x
Editorial	390	Editorial	390	Editorial	390
Radio	391	Radio	391	Radio	391
Politics	392	Politics	392	Politics	392
Brisbane's column	393	Brisbane's column	393	Bob Davis' Column	393
Will Rogers	394	Will Rogers	394	Pittsburghesque by Deuver	394
Sidewalks of Pittsburgh—Boyle	395	Sidewalks of Pittsburgh—Boyle	395	Way of World by Patterson	395
How to Keep Well—Copeland	396	How to Keep Well—Copeland	396	Edgar A. Guest Poem	396
Garrett P. Servias Says	397	Garrett P. Servias Says	397	Tea Talk by Margot Sherman	397
Dr. Frank Crane's column	398	Dr. Frank Crane's column	398	Shopping with Polly	398
O. O. McIntyre	399	O. O. McIntyre	399	Auction Bridge by Work	399
Meditations of a Married Woman— Helen Rowland	39x	Meditations of a Married Woman— Helen Rowland	39x	How to Keep Well by Dr. W. A. Evans	39x
Colored Comic Section	400	Color Rotogravure	400	Letters to Editor	400
Other features (p)	40..	American Weekly	401	Other features (p)	40..
		Automobile Section	402		
		Joke Page	403		
		Other features (p)	40..		
6. Double check (in Q. 5) the ONE feature of GREATEST interest: (a)		6. Double check (in Q. 5) the ONE feature of GREATEST interest: (a)		6. Double check (in Q. 5) the ONE feature of GREATEST interest: (a)	
....	41..	....	41..	....	41..
....	42..	....	42..	....	42..
....	43..	....	43..	....	43..
CARD 4....... X	454	CARD 5....... X	455	CARD 6....... X	456

FIG. 58
An example of a very detailed precoded questionnaire

steps in determining this, because each additional subclassi-
fication makes additional reports necessary. For example,
five hundred carefully distributed reports might show the
proportion of homes with radios for a fairly large city.
If radio ownership were to be worked out by brands, a
larger number of reports would be necessary. If each make
of radio were to be subdivided into price classes, still more
reports would be required. (The principle of sampling is
discussed in Chapter IV.)

A few of the factors which influence the number of
interviews necessary for a reliable sample are:

1. *Scope of investigation.* A national investigation requires more replies than a local one, but not proportionally
more.

2. *Classifications.* If the answers may be influenced by
geographical, urban, rural, social, financial, or similar
factors, more replies are necessary so that each subclassi-
fication will have enough replies to make conclusions about
it reliable.

3. *Reasons for use.* If the reasons for the use of a
product are required, as well as knowledge of its use, the
number of replies will be increased, of course, and each
reason causes a separate classification for tabulation.

4. *Dependent questions.* When a series of questions are
dependent, each upon those preceding it, numerous subdivisions grow up.

5. *Checking.* If, for example, mail questionnaire results
are to be checked by personal interviews, two methods are
being used and the replies from each must be sufficiently
numerous to make each tabulation reliable.

Surveys are valueless unless the results can be depended
upon. A loosely constructed questionnaire may require an
undue number of classifications, thus calling for many
more returns that were obtained. The facts to be found
must be analyzed in detail from this angle before the questionnaire is used. Precoding makes such an analysis obliga-

tory. It should, however, be done just as fully whatever form of tabulation is to be used.

The Tabulating Machine.—Punched cards are placed in the tabulating machine, which quickly sorts them according to any single punch or any combination of punches. When the cards are completely punched, any tabulation or cross tabulation can quickly be worked out. The sorting work is completely taken over by the machine. Accuracy and speed are both obtained.

Question 3: Which brands of Y sell best?

	1st	2nd	3rd	4th	Total Score
Brand A...........	90	200	50	20	1170
Brand B...........	80	220	10	40	1120
Brand C...........	50	200	50	60	1010
Brand D...........	31	109	78	35	673
Brand E...........	30	86	91	32	622
Brand F...........	10	53	57	46	369

FIG. 59

(1st choice counts 5; 2nd choice, 3; 3rd choice, 2; 4th choice, 1.) A preference tabulation.

A comparison of the total scores indicates the relative salability of each brand in the territory investigated. For example, Brand A has about three times the salability of Brand F

Tabulating machines are expensive. They can, however, be rented at a reasonable figure. In addition, companies which own and operate them have grown up in the large cities. The better firms in this business take the coded questionnaires, punch the cards, and tabulate as directed, guaranteeing accurate work.

Types of Tabulation.—There are a number of possible methods of tabulating. Choice among these is determined by the nature of the question and of the answer received. The more common types of tabulation are given on page 206.

1. *One alternative.* The tabulation of questions which may be answered "Yes" or "No" presents the simplest problem.

2. *Order of merit or importance.* When a question is asked which can be answered in more than two ways, the results are recorded according to the frequency with which each possible answer occurs. The answer occurring most often is placed first. An example is given in Fig. 59 on page 205.

3. *Preferences.* When a number of answers are given by each respondent, these answers may be rated for tab-

Brand	1st Choice		2nd Choice		3rd Choice		Total Value
	No. Response	Weighted Value—5	No. Response	Weighted Value—3	No. Response	Weighted Value—1	
X....	5	25	4	12	10	10	47
Y....	6	30	8	24	15	15	69
Z.....	9	45	3	9	5	5	59

FIG. 60
Example showing expression of preferences for particular brands

ulation. For example, in expressing preference for particular brands, five points might be given for first choice, four points for second choice, three for third choice, two for fourth choice, and one for fifth choice. Fig. 60 illustrates this method.

4. *Numerical replies.* To obtain answers to the questions of "How much?" "How many?" or "How often?" the replies are averaged in a number of ways. The arithmetical mean, the mode, or the median are commonly used. Fig. 61 illustrates the use of these.

Cross-analysis.—Simple tabulation often fails to bring out essential facts. For example, 3,000 replies from users might indicate that economy, convenient size, and attractive container were of equal importance as reasons for purchasing a certain product. If respondents were arranged according to income groups, the results might be quite different, the low-income group showing preference because of economy and convenient size, and the high-income group because of the attractive container. Cross-analysis would here show a different picture from that presented by simple tabulation.

How often does the average person use X-brand?

1 Use Every—Days	2 No. of Answers	3 %	1X2
2	100	40.0	200
1	50	20.0	50
3	34	13.6	102
7	20	8.0	140
11 and over	17	6.8	187
4	10	4.0	40
6	8	3.2	48
8	5	2.0	40
9	5	2.0	45
5	3	1.2	15
10	3	1.2	30
	250	100%	897

FIG. 61

Illustration showing use of the arithmetical mean, the mode and the median to obtain answers to such questions as "How much?" "How many?" or "How often?"

Cross tabulations are often based upon characteristics of the unit of observation. For example, income, size of business, nationality, social position, or age might be used for analyzing facts gathered from individuals. Geographical arrangement is also a very usual method of subdividing tabulations. Special classifications are made for cross-analysis whenever necessary. In this connection, it must be remembered that the more minute the subdivisions the fewer cases will fall within their limits, thus lessening the trustworthiness of conclusions drawn from them.

A cross-analysis or cross tabulation based upon brand

TABLE No. 4B

ANALYSIS OF BRAND COMBINATIONS HANDLED BY THE VARIOUS DEALERS

(Importance of dealer according to volume of his cement business arbitrarily rated and indicated as follows: Very Large, Large, Medium, and Small)

	Very large		Large		Medium		Small		Total
	No.	%	No.	%	No.	%	No.	%	
Handling 4 brands or more, incl. A......	5	10.87	22	47.83	18	39.13	1	2.17	(46)
Handling 4 brands or more not incl. A...	4	10.81	23	62.16	9	24.33	1	2.70	(37)
Handling 4 brands or more not incl. B....	2	6.25	17	53.12	11	34.38	2	6.25	(32)
Handling 4 brands or more not incl. C...			14	58.34	10	41.66			(24)
Handling numerous brands, excl. A, B, and C..........	3	15.79	6	31.58	7	36.84	3	15.79	(19)
Dealers handling A only.............	1	7.69	1	7.69	9	69.24	2	15.38	(13)
Dealers handling B only.............			1	5.56	10	55.55	7	38.99	(18)
Dealers handling C only.............					8	57.15	6	42.85	(14)
Dealer handling one or two (not over 2) miscellaneous brands..........			4	14.28	17	60.72	7	25.00	(28)

FIG. 62
An example of a cross tabulation or cross analysis

combinations handled by various dealers is shown in Fig. 62.

Computation.—The mathematical approach to research has been indicated in Chapter IV, "Market Analysis." The use of percentages, index numbers, and correlations follows

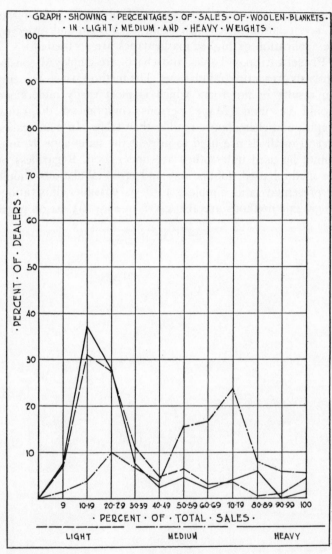

FIG. 63

Graphic chart showing percentages of sales of woolen blankets in
light, medium, and heavy weights

standard mathematical practice, and all data which appear to have relationships which could be clarified and tested by the application of higher mathematics are so treated.

Presentation.—Tables and charts are employed consistently in presenting tabulations. The method which presents the results in the form which is most easily understood should be used. Many persons comprehend diagrams, graphs, and charts more readily than tables. In many cases, several methods are used to present the same data. Results cannot be used unless they are understood. Regardless of the method used, tabulations and cross-tabulations should be presented in as simple a form as possible. Illustrations of graphic methods are also given in Figs. 63, 64 on pages 209, 211.

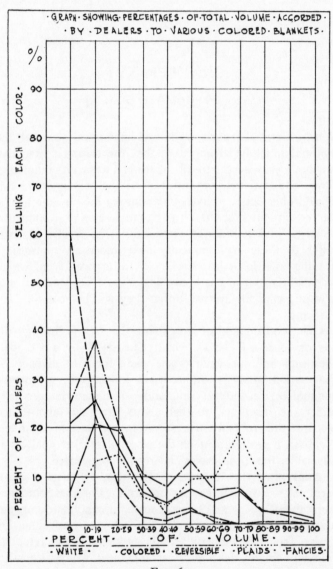

FIG. 64

Graphic chart showing percentages of total volume accorded by
dealers to various colored blankets

CHAPTER XVI

DRAFTING THE REPORT

WHEN the field reports are in and have been tabulated, the material must be arranged so that the research executive can have easy access to all available facts. The tabulation shows the statistical organization of the primary data collected. This can be conveniently summarized by the use of the recapitulation sheets (Fig. 65 on page 213). Comments, remarks, and summaries often cannot be treated statistically; so these are frequently filed under an appropriate heading in a loose-leaf notebook. References from which secondary material has been taken should be systematically kept in a card file system so that they will be accessible for checking.

One good method of organizing the data is through the use of loose-leaf books which take 8½″ by 11″ paper. Headings and subheadings are made for each division of the market analysis. Appropriate tabulations, comments, summaries, secondary data, and other material are filed under the headings, so that all of the facts about each phase of the problem are presented in one place in organized form. If a realignment of the original market analysis is advisable, the loose leaves can readily be shifted.

Analyzing the Tabulated Results.—Statistical treatment takes the facts as they appear on the questionnaires, sums them up, classifies them, etc. If variations occur, analysis of these must be made before any conclusions are drawn from the tabulations. Reclassification and retabulation will finally develop an arrangement which is mathematically consistent in most cases. For example; classifying

Tabulation of replies to each question are given
in the following tables

Question 1: Do you own a radio?

| Yes | 94 | 92.2% |
| No | 8 | 7.8% |

| Total | 102 | 100.0% |

Question 2: If you own a radio, is it a battery or "electric" set?

| Electric | 83 | 88.3% |
| Battery | 11 | 11.7% |

| Total | 94 | 100.0% |

Question 3: If you own a radio, what make is it?

Atwater Kent	22	22.6%
Majestic	15	15.4%
R. C. A.	7	7.2%
Spartan	6	6.2%
Crosley	6	6.2%
Zenith	3	3.1%
Philco	3	3.1%
Kolster	3	3.1%
Victor	3	3.1%
Bosch	2	2.0%
Apex	2	2.0%
Peerless Courier	2	2.0%
Distant-Tone	2	2.0%
Airline	2	2.0%
Brunswick	2	2.0%
Silver Tone	2	2.0%
Home-made	2	2.0%
Fada	1	1.0%
North Star	1	1.0%
Steinite	1	1.0%
Clarion	1	1.0%
Glori-Tone	1	1.0%
Kellogg	1	1.0%
Knight	1	1.0%
King	1	1.0%
Temple	1	1.0%
West-Rad	1	1.0%
Stromberg-Carlson	1	1.0%
G.-M.	1	1.0%
Grebe	1	1.0%
Don't know	1	1.0%

| Total | 98* | 100.0% |

*More than one radio in a few homes.

FIG. 65

A recapitulation sheet which summarizes the tabulated information

housewives by age rather than by income groups might eliminate inconsistency in the case of a particular survey. Some variations, however, cannot be explained so easily. If one town shows twice as great a consumption of a product per 1,000 inhabitants as that shown by all other towns, this must be explained. The variation might be due to increased advertising in the large-consumption town, to the interviewer used there, to the type of population, to unusual dealer support, etc. Before interpretation of the tabulations can honestly be done, all such unusual variations should be studied. In this, comments of the respondents and the interviewers' summaries are of great value.

Comments and Summaries.—Comments and summaries show trends, opinions, and causes. If comments and summaries conflict with the tabulation, the situation must be analyzed and, if necessary, further facts found. For example, a recent survey indicated that brand X was stocked by most stores in a large community. The number of dealers carrying X was twice that of those carrying the brand Y which ranked second. Comments and summaries, however, continually emphasized Y and Z brands in contrast to X. Further investigation showed that X brand was the oldest, and, a few years previous, the best. Brands Y and Z, however, were new and better at the time of the survey. The actual facts were that Y and Z were displacing X, the tabulation showing the present situation, while the comments and summaries showed the trend. Either alone was incomplete, but the interpretation of the two together gave exactly what was desired. Thus the tabulation must be considered along with the comments and summaries.

Clarity of Terms Used.—The research director may delegate many of his functions during the course of the survey and tabulation. The data will finally come to him in finished form. As a result, certain definitions, classifications, and comparisons will already have been made. Great care should be taken to see that the definitions are concise and appear where they are used. The classifications and comparisons should be similarly treated, so that all possible chance of misunderstanding of tabulations and facts may be eliminated. The definitions, classifications, and comparisons should be so clear and concise that an outsider could go over the material without asking any question as to the arbitrary limitations.

Processes of Logic.—There are three main types of reasoning—analogy, induction, and deduction. All of these are used in determining conclusions in research, and they are briefly discussed below.

1. *Analogy.* It is natural in research work to reason that the results from a certain course of action in one particular case will also follow in another apparently similar case. For example, manufacturer X has prospered since his national advertising campaign; therefore his competitor, Y, would prosper by a similar campaign. This example of reasoning by analogy *might* be true if both X and Y sold packaged merchandise of equal value by similar distributive methods. If, however, Y sold bulk goods, it would be very likely untrue. Reasoning by analogy is sound only when the similarity between the two particular cases is demonstrable and sufficient. Otherwise it is easy to make the mistake of comparing cases which are similar only superficially.

2. *Induction.* Induction concludes that what is true of certain members of a class is true of the whole class. If a number of Class C housewives in a city are interviewed, tabulation might show that the main reason for buying X product was economy. This conclusion, based upon information from only part of the housewives of Class C, might be applied to the whole class by induction. The obvious danger is that a sufficiently large and representative portion of the whole group may not be included to make the reasoning by induction correct. An adequate sample is requisite to avoid error.

3. *Deduction.* The deductive method takes a general law and applies it to a particular case. The method is sound, but it is very easy to forget to allow for peculiarities of the particular case to which the general rule is applied. For example, a general survey might determine that local newspapers are the best media for advertising a certain product. Therefore, if it were desired to advertise this product in territory Y, deduction would point to using the local newspapers. But territory Y may be urban or rural, or the population may be predominately white or black. Care must be taken to ascertain that the particular case fits the class to which it is assigned, or the conclusion must be qualified to allow for peculiarities of the individual case.

Fallacies to Be Avoided.—The possibilities of faulty reasoning are numerous. The most important fallacies are enumerated by Jean F. Carroll of the Meredith Publishing Company in the following manner :[1]

1. *Fallacies resulting from inaccurate observation.*
    a. Assuming as a cause something which is merely another effect of the cause.
    b. Assuming as a cause something which, as far as can be determined, is associated with the effect merely by chance.
    c. Assuming as a cause something which is not a cause but simply an antecedent of the effect.
    d. Assuming as a cause something which actually operates after the effect has actually been obtained.
    e. Assuming as a cause something which is a partial cause of the effect, but which is alone inadequate to produce the effect.

2. *Fallacies resulting from inaccurate reasoning process.*
    a. Begging the question or confusing cause and effect.
    b. Hasty generalization.
    c. Fake analogies.
    d. Reasoning in a circle.

[1] *Standards of Research*, by J. F. Carroll, Director Bureau of Market Analysis, Meredith Publishing Company.

Mr. Carroll suggests the following questions as excellent tests to avoid faulty reasoning:

1. Are the facts sufficient to warrant the inference?
2. In case it is not possible or practical to examine all the facts, has care been taken for the spot test?
3. Is there no further inference which could be logically reached from consideration of the facts?
4. Have other and presumably important facts been left out of consideration?
5. Is the apparent connection between the facts and the inference fundamental or is it merely incidental?
6. Is the inference drawn from the consideration of too few instances or from those which are not truly representative?
7. Is the inference partly but not wholly true?

Reasoning in Practical Market Research.—The most common method of reasoning in market research is to make an inference—for example, that a certain method of distribution is best for a particular company—and then gather the facts to prove or disprove the assumption. If there are four possible methods of distribution open to the company, for example, each one of these would have to be handled in this manner. Care must be taken to avoid the assumption that, because one thing is not true, the opposite is true. The inferences which are made really serve only as a structure around which to organize the facts which are gathered. When all of the available data are organized, the research executive studies them and mulls over his problems. If adequate time is available and competent associates are willing to help in interpreting complicated facts, the answer to each problem will finally become clear. In order to obtain reliable conclusions, it is advisable to allow as much time for tabulation, analysis, and report writing as for the field work.

The drawing of conclusions from the assembled data should never be done by one man. Two or more executives should go over the material independently, harmonizing their disagreements after each has reached his own conclusions. In this way, false reasoning and inferences are to a great extent eliminated.

Verification of Conclusions.—Regardless of how carefully conclusions have been deduced from the facts, every effort must be made to test them. The following practical methods are in general use today:

Question 5: Why do you prefer X brand?

	Mail Questionnaire	Personal Interview
Reason A	71%	69%
Reason B	20	15
Reason C	5	12
All others	4	4

The mail questionnaires were used in rural regions and the personal interviewing done in urban sections. Apparently, as regards the reasons for using X, the same facts are of approximately equal importance in both types of community.

FIG. 66

Duality of method is a check on accuracy. The information from the mail questionnaire checks with that from personal interviews, indicating that the facts are dependable

1. *Check controls.* The use of check controls consists in comparing results obtained from two (or more) different field methods (see Fig. 66). For example, personal interviews and mail questionnaires might be used, and the results checked against one another. General Motors Corporation tends to favor this method and sometimes goes even further, checking the facts obtained by its own research department against those found by some outside agency. This method, if carried to its logical conclusion, requires two (or more) independent investigations by

PROBLEM OF THE
BLANK MANUFACTURING COMPANY

The Blank Manufacturing Company, an old concern with excellent resources, has been manufacturing steel products requiring forging, stamping, machining and heat treating in their plant, which is located within 50 miles of New York City. A circumstance has arisen which makes nearly their entire plant, and personnel (including an excellent manufacturing, engineering, and financial organization and about 700 high grade mechanics) available for manufacturing another line of products.

If possible, they would like to make a product which has a ready demand and its primary market within comparatively short shipping distance from New York City.

The product should preferably be made of steel, either forged or stamped; and should preferably require machining. It could also be a product requiring heat treatment. Assembly operations could be performed in the plant.

If necessary, the Blank Manufacturing Company would be willing to buy out from one to three manufacturers in order to reduce competition and obtain an existing distributing system, as well as patterns, special machinery, etc.

The company does not desire to do any product development work, but wants a product which has already passed the development stage; and which has actually been manufactured and sold.

Problem: In what manner should the Blank Manufacturing Company determine the product to manufacture? What concerns have you in mind which appear to meet the above requirements for merger or purchase by the Blank Manufacturing Company?

Note: If the contribution of any individual seems to Percival White, Inc., to warrant it, we will pay him a reward of $100.00.

FIG. 67

A referendum to experts. One method of verifying conclusions is to present a summary of the facts to experts for their opinions

different people and different methods until independent conclusions have been reached by each.

2. *Referendum.* The referendum method is to send copies of the conclusions to different people who are qualified to judge them. In some cases a summary of the facts is sent instead of the conclusions (see Fig. 67 on page 219). Most experts are willing to go over and criticize the submitted material rather carefully in return for the privilege of learning the latest facts. Some surveys are of too confidential a nature to allow the use of this type of verification, yet it is sometimes the only method possible.

3. *Checking.* Errors are very likely to be detected if additional people go over the survey from internal situation analysis to conclusions. Skilled field investigators are useful for this. Many persons can criticize when they cannot create, and two or three independent critical revisions make a fine test.

4. *Trial and error.* Frequently the results of a survey can be tested by actual application to a limited extent before they are generally applied. Trial campaigns, test selling, couponed advertisements, and numerous similar methods are used. Even if the conclusions of the survey are thus completely verified, additional data of sufficient value to warrant the experiment are usually obtained.

The Practical Recommendations.—Many excellent research investigations have resulted in sound conclusions which were never used because they were not embodied in practical business recommendations which could be adopted. If the research executive is unable to offer practical suggestions drawn from his conclusions, an experienced business man should be called in to assist. There are no fixed rules about interpreting facts and formulating business policies. The recommendations must, however, be warranted by the available facts and be adapted to fit the conditions of the particular business for which the research was undertaken. Likewise, they must be so framed as to "sell" themselves to the business executives to whom they will be presented. Facts and conclusions are valueless unless they result in the creation and adoption of more efficient business policies.

Presenting the Report.—Writing the report is important. The presentation must be interesting, logical, and convincing. The report is useless unless the reader is forced to admit the truth of the facts collected, the conclusions drawn, and the recommendations made. The critical reader's viewpoint must be considered throughout. Care also must be taken that the research attitude does not make the presentation too dry, or the report may be relegated to the files without proper consideration. In many cases, the more concise and graphic the presentation of the material can be, the better.

The organization of material in a research report has become somewhat standardized. The following organization is suggested by Professors A. G. Saunders and C. R. Anderson of the University of Illinois, and applies to all formal business reports :[1]

FORMAL REPORTS

    I. Cover.
   II. Title page.
  III. Copyright notice.
  IV. Letter of authorization.
   V. Letter of acceptance.
  VI. Letter of transmittal.
 VII. Letter of approval.
VIII. Table of contents.
  IX. Table of charts and illustrations.
   X. Foreword.
  XI. Preface.
 XII. Acknowledgment.
XIII. Synopsis.

[1] *Business Reports*, by A. G. Saunders and C. R. Anderson, McGraw-Hill Book Company, 1929.

XIV. Body.
      a. Introduction.
      b. Text.
      c. Conclusions and recommendations.
 XV. Appendix.
XVI. Index.

INFORMAL REPORTS

   I. Letter of transmittal.
  II. Purpose or object, and methods.
 III. Conclusions.
 IV. Recommendations.
  V. Supporting details.
 VI. Appendix.

CHAPTER XVII

THE DETECTION OF ERROR

IN MARKET research accuracy is of prime importance. Conclusions can be of no greater accuracy than the facts upon which they are based. Every emphasis is placed upon collecting actual facts and using sound logic to draw conclusions. The foremost guide in this is common sense applied according to the following rules:

1. Are all of the facts and conclusions reasonable?
2. Is the information specific—dates, persons, etc.?
3. Are the data adequate?
4. Do the facts prove the conclusions?
5. Do several different people reach the same conclusions from the data?

Throughout the survey, all facts or conclusions which appear to be unusual should be questioned. "Is this reasonable?" is an important guide to the research director.

Bias.—Bias (that is, prejudice or preconceived opinion) often causes incorrect information to be obtained. A question which suggests an answer will often draw the suggested reply. "To keep up with the Joneses" may be the reason for purchasing an expensive automobile, but the owner is not likely to admit it. Interviewers, if the purpose of the field work is known, may attempt to get results which they believe their employer desires. Bias may occur anywhere and really is an absence of complete impartiality.

If any of the research personnel—investigators, executives, etc.—have a positive opinion about the facts before they are obtained, they will unconsciously attempt to prove that opinion.

Prevention of bias is difficult. The best method to avoid it is to have two or more people perform independently the same function, like drawing conclusions, and to gather facts by two or more distinct methods, as by personal interview and mail questionnaire. Likewise, questionnaires are tested; interviewers are sometimes left in ignorance of the specific purpose of the survey; indirect questions are asked consumers; known prejudices are allowed for; conclusions are tested; etc.

Compensating and Cumulative Errors.—Compensating errors are those which cancel one another as an increasing number of interviews or items is obtained. Cumulative errors are those which keep piling up regardless of how many additional cases or items are added. Ten out of every hundred consumers in a certain city may use X product. If a thousand interviews were made, the first hundred might give fifteen users, the second hundred eight users, etc. As each additional hundred interviews is added, the error becomes less because some errors are plus and some are minus—*i.e.,* the errors compensate. This fact makes it necessary to be sure the sample is adequate.

Cumulative errors are those which always fall on the plus (or minus) side. For example, the question, "Do you read *Vogue*?" would be answered in the positive by far too many housewives. *Vogue* is an expensive magazine not bought by the great bulk of women, yet its authority in style and fashion is such that most women willingly admit reading it if such a direct question is asked.

The great importance of eliminating bias is because it almost invariably results in errors of the cumulative type. If bias is not detected, it is bound to affect conclusions and recommendations, and every known means should be used to avoid its occurrence.

Errors on the Part of Respondents.—Respondents sometimes give inconsistent answers. One question may be unanswered. One answer may appear unreasonable. The respondent may be taking the interview as a joke and be "kidding." In such cases, some sort of checking must be done or the doubtful statements thrown out. Second calls or recalls are sometimes made when the data are incomplete or contradictory. "Funny" responses should be eliminated. In the case of mail questionnaires, a letter asking for verification of the first answers may be sent.

When the respondents are apparently giving biased answers, an indirect method of questioning may be used to determine the existence of bias and its approximate amount. Actual magazine circulations may, for example, be also employed to check results.

In personal interviewing, error on the part of respondents must be checked before the investigator leaves the locality. Interviews must be examined before they are sent to the central office and every effort must be made to leave no loose ends which will require a return trip.

Faking by Interviewers.—Faking by an interviewer is hard to prevent if he really desires to deceive. Care in choosing field investigators is its best preventive. "Know your field workers" is a primary rule. In general, unskilled investigators should always be closely supervised because, as temporary workers, they have little interest in the success of the survey.

The nature of the questionnaire has a great deal to do with faking. If simple facts alone are recorded, variation in the replies is limited. An investigator with two hundred consumer interviews to report can make fifty calls and spread the results of these over the one hundred and fifty faked reports of calls which were not made. As the complexity of the questionnaire increases through the inclusion of personal experience with the product, suggested improvements, reasons for use, etc., faking becomes more difficult and burdensome. If comments and remarks are insisted upon, in addition, it may be easier to make interviews than to fake the reports, because the variations which occur in the actual interviews can be mentally created, beyond a certain point, only with the greatest difficulty. In addition, requiring specific information about each respondent—age, address, occupation, etc.—makes the creation of an imaginary respondent still harder.

Supervising Interviewers.—The use of unskilled investigators is practically limited to interviewing consumers. A supervisor escorts a number of these workers through a residential section or an office building. He closely watches over the group and examines the reports soon after their completion. The procedure is somewhat like that used in a house-to-house magazine subscription canvass. Faking is precluded to a great extent by this method.

People are more likely to be honest when in association with others than when alone. When semi-skilled and skilled investigators are working without direct supervision, grouping them together in pairs or other units, often will greatly lessen the number of fictitious reports. Also, having two or more interviewers work at different times in the same locality and class of respondents tends to increase accuracy. Not only is faking thus greatly lessened, but the existence of bias on the part of interviewers is likely to be discovered.

Checking up on Interviewers.—Most questionnaires require some identification of the respondent—name, address, business, automobile license number, or the like. Only in the case of consumers is this information difficult to obtain. With such data, checking can be done on all respondents or on a sample group. Several methods are common:

1. *Telephone checking.* When the identification data include the respondents' telephone numbers, a large number of calls can be quickly and cheaply made to determine

PERCIVAL WHITE
INCORPORATED
MARKETING COUNSELORS
25 WEST 45ᵀᴴ STREET
NEW YORK
CABLES-DEDDIKRA

March 16, 1931.

Dear Miss (Mrs.)   B l a n k --

　　We appreciate your kindness in helping one of
our interviewers to obtain some information about
cosmetic needs and habits and particularly about
Ambrosia.

　　Since we are very anxious that all our reports
should be accurate in every respect, will you please
check the information below?

　　We enclose a stamped, addressed envelope, and
should be grateful for your reply.

　　　　　　　　　Yours faithfully,

　　　　　　　　　PERCIVAL WHITE, INC.

Miss -----

　　　　　I have been interviewed

　　　　.I have not been interviewed

　　　　　(Underline, please)

FIG. 68
A standard check-up letter to verify the validity of interviews. This
organization always checks upon a survey in this manner

whether the reports are real or fictitious. A small number of these telephone calls can request verification of the information written on the questionnaire.

2. *Mail questionnaire checking.* A mail questionnaire may be sent to personal-interview respondents. This, for example, may thank the person for his coöperation in the interview, request approval of the report of the interview (a copy being inclosed), and ask one additional question. A stamped and addressed return envelope should, of course, be inclosed. Additional questions asked by mail may be necessary, or they may be merely devices for checking. Fig. 68 on page 227 shows a standard check-up letter used.

3. *Personal-interview checking.* In some cases, a second call is made upon a small number of respondents, usually selected by chance, to check the accuracy of the original reports. The supplementary question technique is often used in this procedure.

Checking Secondary Sources.—All information which is not collected first hand comes from what are called secondary sources. The most common of these sources are books, magazines, survey reports, and company records. This material should be subjected to the same rigid examination that is given to data collected in the field. Some useful criteria for judging such information are:

1. Is the authority dependable?
2. Is the authority up-to-date?
3. Is the authority supported by other authorities? In conflict with them?
4. Is there evidence to believe that the applicable material was considered significant by the authority?
5. Can the conclusions of the authority be tested? Have they been tested?

INDEX

Reilly, W. J., 114
Reliability, 59
Remarks, 212
Repetition, 157
Replacements, future, 146
Replies, numerical, 206
Reports, drafting, 212
 field, 123
 formula, 221
 informal, 222
 mailing, 162
 presenting, 221
 survey, 10
Representativeness, 59
Research, agencies, types of, 14
 bibliographical, 178
 demand for, 17
 department, 21
  advertising agency, 18
  organization of, 16
 field, application of, 25
 organizations, 5
  commercial, 20
 processes of, 58
Resident, field force, 116
 investigators, 85
Residential, sections, 134
Respondents, classification of, 136
 "doubtful," 146
 errors on part of, 225
 habits of prospective, 136
Response, 83
Restricted calls, 135
Results, analyzing, 212
 application of, 63
 uniformity of, 129
Retailers, interviewing, 148
Retailing, 112
Returns, analysis of, 51
 mail, 11
Rewards, 165, 190
Ronald Press, 114
Routing, 122, 135
 economical, 136
Rugs, 31
Rules, editing, 195
 for questionnaire, 182
 for recording, 152

Sales, force, 91
 use of, 98
 records, 98
 repeat, 40
Salesmen, as interviewers, 170
 limitations, 100
Sample, validity of, 75
Samples, 165
Sampling, 35, 52, 200
 principle of, 204
 reliable, 204
Saunders, Prof. A. G., 221
Scientific management, 4
Sections, residential, 134
Selling, test, 170
Sequence toll-call plan, 87
Service, 21
Sex, 60
Sheet, expense, 125
 master, 125
 recapitulation, 213
Situations, internal, 177
 survey, 64
 local, 133
Slogans, 41
Sources, checking secondary, 228
 of field personnel, 112
Specified, list, 147
Standard Oil Co. of Indiana, 169
Standards of Research, 67, 140, 216
Statistical, approach, 52
 department, 60
Sterling, John C., 24
Stewart Warner Speedometer Corp., 15
Students, 113
Study, situation, 64
Style, trends, 31
Summary, 123, 158, 212, 214
 amplification of, 163
 facts included in, 160
 first class, 159
 investigator judged by, 162
 purposes of, 159
 reporters' daily, 161
 use of, 160